THE TONGUE: A FORCE OF LIFE OR DEATH

By

DANIELLE RICHARDSON

© 2018
Published by Parables

All rights reserved. No part of this book may be reproduced in any form by any electronic or mechanical means (including photocopying, recording, or information storage and retrieval) without permission in writing from the publisher, except for reading and browsing via the World Wide Web. Users are not permitted to mount this file on any network servers.

All scripture quotations are taken from the King James Version of the Holy Bible

Edited by Ami Shirley, Melanie Dean and Frankie Mitchell

Compilation and formatting by Michael Richardson

Printed and Bound in the United States of America

Acknowledgements

I am very grateful to my two friends and my mother who painstakingly edited this book for me. Thanks to Ami Shirley, Melanie Dean and Frankie Mitchell. I couldn't have done it without you.

I want to thank my husband for helping with the story illustration at the beginning of each chapter and formatting the manuscript.
Love you, honey!

I am so proud of my two children who are seeking to serve God and I pray that they will keep Jesus first in their lives. I love you, Andrea and James. I thank God for blessing me with you.

I am also blessed to have an encouraging mother, Frankie Mitchell. She has been there for us through the tough times in ministry and encouraging me to share this message with others.

My brothers, Randy and Steve, and my sister, Susan, have been encouraging to me throughout the writing process. I want to express a special thanks to my brother, Steve, who has now gone to be with Lord, for sharing my book with others. I love you all.

I wish to thank the pastors' wives who have shared their personal challenges and experiences which have helped fuel the need for this teaching and for their encouragement and prayers toward this project.

Most importantly, I want to thank the Lord for being our Strength while we were experiencing much of what is in this book. Through the pain and heartache we have seen God's wonderful grace and mercy. God's Hand has led us through the fires to help be a blessing to the many ministers and their wives who are on the front lines of ministry and deal with similar heartaches each day.

For more information about my ministry, please email me at: encouragingpastorswives@gmail.com. My desire is to encourage women, especially ministers' wives.

You can listen to my radio segment "Encouraging Words for Ministers' Wives" online at www.KELBradio.com..

You are also welcome to email me to share stories or to make comments about this book.

Find me on Instagram@encouragingministerswives
You Tube: Danielle Richardson

TABLE OF CONTENTS

Introduction

Chapter 1
The Culprit

Chapter 2
Whispering Saints

Chapter 3
The Spirit of Offense

Chapter 4
Sowing Seeds of Discord

Chapter 5
Under The Influence

Chapter 6
Inside The Parsonage

Chapter 7
Having Done All, Stand

Epilogue

THE TONGUE, A FORCE OF LIFE OR DEATH

Introduction

I am the wife of a pastor, and my husband and I have been a ministry team for about 20 years. We worked in youth and music ministry before entering the pastorate. Throughout the years, we have come into contact with many types of church members. Some experiences with these members have been positive, some negative and some just plain scary. There have been calm moments, but others have been a rollercoaster ride. At times, we have been accepted, loved, embraced and protected. In other instances, we have been knocked down, cursed, threatened, insulted and criticized.

As I look back throughout my journey as a minister's wife, I realize that God has been preparing me all along for this moment. I feel that God is leading me to encourage and to assist women and pastor's wives. At times, I have wondered why I was going through those difficult times. There is great peace in now knowing what God wants me to do and that is to encourage women, especially pastor's wives.

The message I value most about those dark moments in the wilderness of ministry is that God brought us out. We made it through by His grace and you will too.

I felt the need to write this book based on some of my experiences and those of fellow pastors' wives. This book is written strictly from the point of view of pastor's wives. Pastors and wives have not arrived. There is no claim that we are perfect or even not part of the problems at times.

This book is to educate and encourage people of the church to be able to recognize the damage that the tongue can do and to tame this deadly force. I also want to use this book as a tool to encourage pastors and their wives, letting them know that someone else understands what they are going through, to realize that God is in control and that there is a light at the end of the tunnel. I want this book to be as if we were sitting together having a heart to heart chat. I am opening my heart to you as I will be sharing things here that I have not shared with anyone.

Dear pastor's wife, be grateful that you have been called out to be an example and to minister to women in your church. I am sure that you will be able to identify with the stories and experiences in this book. You are blessed, even though it doesn't seem like it at times. I pray that this book helps you to know that someone understands and cares.

In case any of you are pastors' wives, I have written a special word to you throughout this book in order to speak directly to you and hopefully to encourage you.

CHAPTER ONE

THE CULPRIT

Bro. Bill was working late in his office touching up the sermon he was preparing to deliver to his congregation the next morning. He was a bit anxious about using just the right words, so as not to have anyone think he was aiming this message directly at them. It was time to preach a message on unity and he couldn't preach about unity without touching on forgiveness. The atmosphere around the church had become a bit thick and he couldn't really put his finger on it. Though nobody had spoken any complaints to him, he couldn't help but feel that there were some undercurrents stirring. Bill and Judy had moved to their new field of service just seven short months earlier. He simply tried to assure himself that the honeymoon stage was over and this was just the normal atmosphere of ministry.

He began to allow his mind to drift with thoughts and images of the good 'ole days when ministry was fun and exciting, from new discoveries to optimistic challenges. It seemed as though criticism simply rolled right off, like water off a duck's back. As he imagined what a church in perfect unity and harmony must look like, he wondered if there was ever a time in history when churches reflected that beautiful picture of unity and joy. He began to get lost in his daydream, as he imagined what it must have been like to pastor a church back in the day when pastors were a leading voice in the church and community. He mused about a day when pastors were treated with respect and admiration.

SLAM! Bill snapped out of his daydream state as fear and sudden panic clinched his heart and mind.

"What was that loud noise? Was someone else here or did something fall?" Bill thought to himself.

It sounded like the outer door down the hall and around the corner.

He quickly rose out of his chair still a bit shaken from being snapped back to reality. He looked around quickly to arm himself as he went to investigate the noise. Unfortunately, all he had available was a stapler and a letter opener. He decided against either and simply uttered a quick prayer while convincing himself that he could handle whatever it was that spooked him.

As he quietly opened the door to his office, he heard the sound of footsteps and then another door close which sounded like the door leading into the sanctuary. He decided to go back to his desk for the letter opener just in case then turned and headed out into the hall with slow quiet steps like a hunter stalking its prey, only Bill felt like he was the prey.

As he cautiously crept down the dimly lit hallway, he could see a faint glow of light coming from beneath the door to the sanctuary. Even though he felt a cold chill, he reasoned with himself that it must simply be someone who forgot something and didn't want to bother him.

He heard a faint noise in the sanctuary and began to step a little quicker to the door leading into the sanctuary. He placed his hand on the door knob and hesitated. He pictured in his mind charging in boldly with authority rather than the fear he was sensing inside. He took a deep breath and prepared to charge in when another noise caught his ear. He heard a motor start up outside, so he hurried to a window to see if he could get a glance of who it was parked outside. He could barely see the tail lights as they sped off down the dark country road.

Feeling a bit more secure, he cautiously headed back toward the sanctuary to see about the light. His hands were trembling and his breathing was loud and heavy as he reached for the door handle. As he went in, he saw that the light over the pulpit had been left on. Looking around to make certain no one else was lingering, he headed over to the light switch to turn it off. On his way a glint caught his eye from some object standing in the center of the pulpit. He turned towards the pulpit to see what was reflecting the light. His heart began to pound so loudly, he could have sworn it was reverberating throughout the auditorium. As each step took him closer to the podium and he climbed the steps to the stage, his heart sank in horror at what he saw. His skin began to crawl up his back, causing his head and hands to tremble. His hands gripped the sides of the pulpit. He couldn't believe his eyes as he blinked to make sure that it was real.

In the center of the pulpit, there was a knife pierced into the wooden surface that held a folded note in place with the word "PREACHER" scribbled on it in capital letters. He stood there for what seemed an eternity just staring at the knife and note. His eyes would dart around the dark auditorium and back to the knife as he began to look at it from every angle. His eyes had to adjust to the light again.

Who could have done such a thing? Who would desecrate the Lord's property? Should I leave it there and call the police or keep quiet and pray about it? All of these questions were racing through Bill's mind.

After debating with himself, Bill decided to remove it and expose what was inside the note.

Bill grabbed the handle of the knife with both hands and with a few wiggles pulled it free. The paper slid down and Bill could see a deep gash in his trusted friend. He couldn't help but feel attached to the piece of furniture as though it were his personal lectern. He instinctively rubbed his finger over the gash in the pulpit still amazed at what he was experiencing.

He opened the note to see what surprise awaited him. It was more than a mere surprise. It was a shock! The note simply read, "Leave our church before we make you leave." It was signed, "A concerned church member."

Wow! Bill didn't see this coming. All he could think about was who exactly made up the "we" in the note. Was it a few people or was it a majority? Bill had only been on the field for seven months and even though he had seen some positive movements in church growth, there simply seemed to be a few who remained detached from his leadership. His family was still making adjustments to the new town and schools. His wife was trying to be the model "Preacher's Wife" without coming between those who had life-long or best friend relationships before they arrived on the field.

Bill felt a sense of hurt, betrayal, anger, frustration and bewilderment within and his legs felt as though they could no longer hold him up. "What have I done to cause this kind of action? Who hates me this much to leave such an awful threat?" he thought. "How will I be able to preach in the morning not knowing who the culprit is? How will I explain this to Judy?" Thoughts raced through his mind of how this action could have gotten this far, and how his wife would react. Would he have to uproot his family again or would he even desire to continue in ministry? He put his head in his hands and sobbed.

The Culprit

Today there are more ministers called of God to lead and serve God's flocks who are bullied, threatened, terminated and sometimes worse, as false accusations slander their character and reputation. This is unfortunate and unnecessary. It doesn't begin with hostility. It actually begins with a single member who cunningly creates such dangerous conditions that can and will bring chaos, rebellion, anger, hatred and even death into the church. It is often aimed at the minister's wife, simply because she is his help mate. Even the children are not immune from vicious attacks that can result in fleeing from serving God and the church when they become adults. It often results in the preacher's kids falling into a life of debauchery as they segregate themselves from the institution that has brought so much pain into their home.

The Tongue is the deadliest force in your church! In this study we will expose it and learn what God's word teaches us in dealing with our words. I want to spare our churches from injury and destroying her reputation in the community and the world.

In conversations among pastors and church leaders, questions continue to arise. Why can't we seem to have more people interested in church today? Why are the younger folks absent from the local church? How can we keep people interested and excited about being a part of the church?

The church today seems to have lost its relevance in the lives of society. The church and its influence is quickly beginning to fade from our national landscape and heritage. Without getting into all the generational and social challenges facing our churches today, which I will leave to the experts, I do want to bring to light a predominate cause of decline in our churches. There are thousands of ministers and families who are grieving because of the member of the body that no man can tame, which is alive and well in every single church causing pain, grief and destruction.

In every church lurks the one thing that causes so much damage to the very name of Christ and the ministries of the church which represent Him. If this could be stopped, then it is likely that a great number of our churches today would not only become healthy and thriving within, but would also become a great witness and attract the lost to the saving grace of our Lord Jesus Christ. After all, isn't that the reason that churches exist?

There's a beautiful song we sing in many churches entitled, *They Will Know Us by Our Love*. Oh, that the churches of God could truly believe and live out those words that we sing.

Think of someone in your church who has hurt you in some way; someone who backbites, tears apart and kills the ministries of the church. I am sure that the face of someone or a group of people has already flashed through your mind. What could be so important that it needs this book written about it? If you think about it for a while, you might ask yourself, "Is it the church busybody or a known bully, a Sunday school teacher, a deacon or elder? Who could this be? Could it even be me?"

I have found through experience and after literally dozens of conversations with other wives of pastors, that there is one member of the church no one can tame. When the tongue gets out of control, there is no stopping it. This deadly force has sent many pastors, their wives, and even their children running to their homes in tears. It has tempted pastors to turn in their resignations on Monday mornings and consider walking away from their call to serve God. This is putting the future state of our churches and God's kingdom work at stake. Out of control, the tongue can contaminate the body of Christ like a plague with no resistance.

A member of the church that causes destruction with their words is so dangerous. The effects may sneak up over a long time period, like a cat waiting to pounce or like an explosion similar to a pressure cooker that builds up pressure quietly until it blows. It may be concealed like a snake in the grass or as obvious as a freight train barreling over the tracks. Of equal danger, it could be someone you thought was your best friend and confidant. This member can affect a church, ministers and members of the church, and it can even creep into your family relationships. Husbands and wives have divorced from the fallout and some have died either through health issues related to the attacks or even the unthinkable, a minister or his spouse taking their own life, unable to cope with the stress and assaults. I have witnessed churches split, torn apart, and devastated. People have been deceived, manipulated and left helpless and bitter in the wake of this member. I have seen people who have intentionally drawn close to the pastor or his wife in order to get close enough to strike. You might be thinking, who in the world could be that destructive? Who would do this to a minister and his family and why is it so common in our churches today? In fact, I will tell you that this member is in every congregation, no matter the denomination or culture.

How can we turn the tide? How would we handle this type of member? Should we ask this person to leave the church to keep peace? Should we show mercy? Maybe we could pray for them, be an example or just simply ignore them. Before we can find the solution, we will need to identify this deadly member of the church.

The <u>tongue</u> of a church member, pastor or staff is the deadliest member of your church. The Bible says in James 3:5 "the tongue is a little member and boasteth great things." And in James 3:8 "that no man can tame the tongue and that it is an unruly evil, full of deadly poison." Even though it is so small, the <u>tongue</u> is the deadliest member of the body. The tongue can sing beautiful and boisterous songs, make great speeches, or preach sermons that change lives. Our tongues can spread joy or pain in an instant. The tongue is necessary for communication and it operates as a direct result of our emotions and our thoughts. Our brain sends impulses to our tongues and we speak. Even back in the Bible days, the tongue was an unruly member of the body. That is why there are so many scriptures about it. If the tongue was trouble then, why wouldn't it be trouble with our generation? Unfortunately, the temptation to misuse our tongues is still prevalent today.

We will see later how the tongue can also destroy relationships between the pulpit and the pews. James 1:26 says, "If any man among you seem to be religious, and bridleth not his tongue, but deceiveth his own heart, this man's religion is in vain." A person can try to fool other people, but they will never fool God. They can seem to be religious, but if they use their tongues for evil, then their witness is in vain. People can hear what you are saying and how you are saying it, and if you have been a bad witness in talking about others, it will show.

Words

Hebrews 11:3 says, "Through faith we understand that the worlds were framed by the word of God, so that things which are seen were not made of things which do appear." This scripture tells me that the Words of God created the world. He formed the entire earth with words. God spoke everything into existence with words, not His Hands or the hands of anyone else. God formed the mountains, trees and clouds with His power-filled words. God spoke day and night into existence and we still have day and night today. Every evening the sun will go down and every morning the sun will rise. That has not changed since God spoke it into being.

We still have mountains, trees and everything that He spoke into existence. It is all still around us today. HOW POWERFUL IS THAT? Think about the enormity and permanence of those words. Words are a product or a result of our tongues and convey our most private thoughts and opinions. Words are permanent. They can be our enemies or our friends. Once words are spoken, they cannot be pulled back into the mouth. Sometimes I have the opportunity to teach our youth class and I brought some tubes of toothpaste and told them to squeeze all of the toothpaste out into a bowl. Then I told them to neatly get the toothpaste back into the tube. As they tried to do that, they got toothpaste all over themselves. It was impossible to get all of that toothpaste back into the tube. Our words are exactly like that tube of toothpaste. After the words are said and they reach the ears of the hearer, it is too late to take them back. Those words have already commanded a response, whether an emotional response within the person, or an audible response from the hearer's lips. Sometimes, the receiver of the words gives no response at all. We can feel remorse and even apologize for those words, and the apology might soothe the person a little, but the damage is already done. There is no "undo" button on the tongue like we have on our computers. Believe me, I have said things that I wish could be sucked back into my mouth in an instant.

Let's imagine a piece of wood. If you hammer nails into the wood and then pull the nails back out, they will leave holes in the wood. You can try to fill the holes with putty, but the holes are still there, just covered up. That is the way words are. Unkind words will leave holes in the hearts of the people to which they are spoken. Sometimes the pain of those words can last a lifetime. If might affect the rest of their lives.

I have seen people say things and regret it instantly and then try to erase the words in the air. That will not take back those words. I have heard people say, "My bad" after saying something they shouldn't, as if that would take away the statement. The best thing is to not say things that we will want to take back. I am writing this book to myself, as well as others. This book has been an eye opener for me also. We will not stop learning and changing until we die.

Words of Death

God did not form words for us to use them against each other. Each one of us has the power of the spoken word. We choose, yes choose, whether we will speak with positive or negative influence. The Bible says in Proverbs 18:2, "there is life and death in the power of the tongue." That is a powerful, but scary statement. We can bring positive or negative thoughts and ideas to a person's life. What power our little tongues have! It is our choice to either lift up or tear down our friends. We can bring suffering and pain or we can bring life, healing and happiness to someone's life. We can practice using our tongues for good. James 3:10 says, "Out of the same mouth proceedeth blessing and cursing. My brethren, these things ought not so to be."

This is where the choice comes in. We do not need to be cursing anyone at any time. I believe that we are supposed to bring blessings to people and to encourage them any time that we can, even in our own homes. Sometimes, folks are nicer to the people who live outside of their homes. We need to show our children and family love also. We need to be what we appear to be out in the public eye and we need to make a conscious effort to speak blessings upon people instead of curses.

Let's examine some sentences that bring death to others. If these sentences were to be spoken to another person, you can almost feel the death and tension that it brings to that person's

spirit. Read the list of horrible statements:
1. I hate you!
2. I wish you were never born!
3. You are ugly!
4. You are so stupid!
5. I don't know why I married you!
6. I don't like you!

How devastatingly hurtful these words are! These sentences are merely words, but when we put those words together, they take on a new meaning that tear down and wound the spirit of another person. We can almost see the wounds that those daggers make in another person and they leave scars. We need to be especially careful of what we say to children and teenagers. Their speaking habits are formed at an early age and we need to build them up and never, ever tear them down. They depend on us to be an example to them and to encourage them in their lives.

Even though we are pastors and pastors' wives, we are human and are not immune to saying the wrong words to someone, whether it be intentionally or unintentionally. We do make mistakes, especially with our tongues. This is a reminder of our human aspects. My tongue has made mistakes and I try to apologize when I feel the conviction to do so. God has taught me many things in this study and I am trying to tame my own tongue. I pray that you will do the same as we study this subject together.

Words of Life

We went to a restaurant a few months ago and the waitress came out with no smile, just a business only expression on her face. I noticed she had pretty teeth, so I mentioned it. At that moment, her entire face lit up and she smiled a beautiful smile that reached her eyes. The kind words that we speak may make the difference between life and death or between others having a good day or a bad one. When I enjoy being around someone, especially church people, I tell them that they are fun to be around. Their faces light up and it makes them feel good about themselves. I try and make it a habit now that I see how much joy it brings to them. Look for things about which to compliment others. After studying the power of words, especially that they bring life to someone, I make a point to tell people how great of a job they are doing or how helpful they are to me. I have noticed with bill collectors that if I start out with a positive tone and be polite to them, they will do whatever they can to help me. If I start out by asking them how they are doing, they usually tell me if they are having a good day or a bad day. If they are having a bad day, I try and encourage them and listen to them. Sometimes I even hear them laugh before the conversation is over.

Sometimes people just need to voice a concern or a frustration, and when they do, they feel better. We need to be there for people and to show love to them. When you speak to a store clerk or a waitress, pretend that what you say is the only positive thing that person hears that day, that week or even that year. It very well may be. I have gotten into the habit of finding something positive to say about people I deal with in business or in restaurants. People need to hear something nice about them.

If we were able to read people's thoughts after harsh words are spoken, we would see that words hurt much more than we ever knew. Also, we would see that just one encouraging word can be the difference of life and death in some cases. Someone could be on the verge of suicide and you might be the last person that they have the opportunity to speak to before they decide.

As I had previously mentioned about my fear of people while I was in school, there was a teenager named Michele whom I saw in the halls every day, sometimes a couple of times a day. She was head cheerleader and I was amazed that she cared enough to smile and say "hi" to me every time I saw her. She didn't even know that I was terrified inside and that her smile and kindness toward me actually helped me. I started looking forward to seeing her in the hallway every day. She still has a smile that lights up her entire face and it brings joy to others. We have become friends and keep in touch and I still feel encouraged by her. She makes me laugh. It is obvious that she has a close relationship with God. She is proof that one person can make a huge difference. Recently, I was grateful to be able to share with her how touched I was by her love of God and others, even when she was a teenager.

Let's read some phrases that bring life to other people:

1. I love you.
2. I am glad that you are in my life.
3. You are pretty.
4. You bring joy to my life.
5. You mean the world to me.
6. You brighten my day.

Proverbs 16:24 says, "Pleasant words are as an honeycomb, sweet to the soul, and health to the bones."

This verse tells us that when we speak positive words, it actually brings health to the bones, whether it is the health of the speaker or the health of the person hearing the words. It makes me feel good that I can bring health to someone's bones with encouraging words. This makes me want to go and encourage more people in my life in order to share the soothing balm of pleasant words.

The most important topic of sharing words of life is to share

Jesus Christ with people and to lead them to a relationship with God. This is the greatest use of our tongues that makes an eternal, forever difference for God's Kingdom!

How to Stay Out of Trouble

During my study, I noticed that in God's Word, He shows us ways to keep our tongues from causing trouble for our souls. Proverbs 21:23 says, "Whoso keepeth his tongue keepeth his soul from troubles." He gives us a solution to the troublesome tongue that we all have at some point in our lives. This scripture speaks of abstaining from speaking especially if we don't have something kind to say.

If we are confessing words about God, then we will avoid many troubles. If we dwell on praiseworthy things of God, then the natural result will be to speak praiseworthy things of God. They will flow forth like a stream refreshing our souls.

Read the following scriptures:

1. In Psalms 119:172, David tells the Lord "My tongue shall speak of Thy Word; for all thy commandments are righteousness." If we speak about the things of God and what is in the Bible, we are speaking life and love to others, which is what God expects of us.
2. Psalms 145:21 says, "My mouth shall speak the praise of the Lord and let all flesh bless His Holy Name forever and ever."
3. Psalms 145:11 "They shall speak of the glory of thy kingdom and talk of thy power."
4. Psalms 145:5 "I will speak of the glorious honour of thy majesty, and of thy wondrous works."

5. Psalms 126:2 says, "Then was our mouth filled with laughter, and our tongue with singing: then said they among the heathen, The Lord hath done great things for them."

If we are praising God with our tongues instead of gossiping, then the lost people will see that God does great things for us. We can be a witness to others because of what they see in us. As we can see by reading these scriptures, if we are concentrating on the things of God and praising God, it will keep our tongues from doing evil deeds. I have gotten into the habit of listening to my headphones with praise music in my ears as I clean the house. It gets my mind off of troubles and makes me feel positive.

Wisdom

There is a connection between a godly tongue and wisdom. Proverbs 31:26 says, "She opened her mouth with wisdom and in her tongue is the law of kindness."

This passage suggests to us that a person who uses wisdom speaks kind sayings to others. Those who often speak words of kindness to others may be perceived as people with wisdom. That's an interesting test to determine who you may seek counsel from. Think of individuals who seem to spread kindness through their words. Those would be the very ones I might consider approaching in times when I might need advice.

In every church we have been associated with, there were people who spoke life to us through their kind words. It warms my heart to hear someone say they are glad to see me or it encourages me whenever someone compliments my piano abilities or something that I have done that had touched their lives in some way. I do not do it for the praise of people, but it makes me feel special. It tells me that I matter and that I have a purpose and effected that purpose into their life which has blessed them. They in return bless me when they show appreciation and encouragement toward me.

Just one positive statement to someone goes a very long way in making them feel good about themselves. One of my dear friends spoke encouragement to me often. She brought light to my life and is still a very dear friend to me and we go and visit her. I loved being around her because she made me laugh. She was naturally funny with no effort. She brings life to others around her and she always spoke words of kindness. To this day, whenever I talk to her on the phone, just the sound of her voice makes me feel happy.

I have a close friend who is a pastor's wife, and she lifts me up with her encouraging words. She prays for me, but most importantly she **tells** me that she is praying for me. She encourages me so much and has made a difference in my life. I also get the opportunity to encourage her and to pray for her also. We are a support to each other because we have been through some of the same experiences.

Psalms 37:30 says, "The mouth of the righteous speaketh wisdom…"

Proverbs 10:31: "the mouth of the just bringeth forth wisdom: but the forward tongue shall be cut out."

Proverbs 12:18 says, "….the tongue of the wise is health."

Proverbs 15:2 says, "The tongue of the wise useth knowledge aright: but the mouth of fools poureth out foolishness."

If a wise person acquires information about someone, then they are very discreet who they share it with, if at all. Because their nature is to encourage and speak kind words they almost never criticize or gossip about others. A foolish person, on the other hand, is not careful with whom that information is shared. Someone who is wise speaks of godly things and doesn't use his or her, tongue to bring destruction and harm to others. This is what we should strive to do. I want to be wise in God's eyes and I am striving to please God with my speech.

I am not perfect and I will continue to make mistakes, but hopefully I will be making fewer of them after studying the power of words. Speaking kind, uplifting words to others must begin as a desire. If you desire to be a person who speaks kindness, then you must practice the discipline of focusing on positive and encouraging words and comments. After a while of practicing this discipline it will then become a delight to speak kindly toward others and you will be a delight for others to be around.

Think Before We Speak

My husband shared this acronym in a recent sermon.

T.H.I.N.K.: A TEST before we Speak!
- **T** - Is it True?
- **H** - Is it Helpful?
- **I** - Is it Inspiring?
- **N** - Is it Necessary?
- **K** - Is it Kind?

Psalms 12:4 says, "With our tongue will we prevail; our lips are our own, who is lord over us?" We can tell who is ruling our bodies and our lives by the very words that come out of our mouths. Our lips are our own and we make our own decisions about what we say and do. Some people think before they speak, while others have a habit of speaking spontaneously.

I have a sweet friend who pauses to think for several seconds before answering. I am trying to learn that trait. She keeps her tongue in check and stays out of trouble. She is a very wise person for doing that. At first, I was a little intimidated by that until I figured out what she was doing. My father was like that also. He was a very quiet and Godly man and he was a very good listener. He didn't speak much, but when he said something, it was something worth hearing. He prayed about things before he spoke and he prayed for people and he was respected in the church and in the community.

Examine Ourselves

Luke 6:45 says, "What you speak comes from the abundance of your heart." What is in your heart eventually comes out of your mouth. As you read this book, please examine yourself to see if you can be a joy to your church and a source of relief from the pain and struggles that careless words bring to your pastor and his family. Just because a thought pops into our heads, it doesn't mean that we need to voice it. I have already mentioned this verse, but it bears mentioning again. Matthew 12:36 says, "But I say unto you, that every idle (or careless) word that men shall speak, they shall give account thereof in the Day of Judgment."

As I am studying this material, I am convicted of how I have used my words during my life. This is a serious matter! It is eye-opening to know that we will be judged on every word that we speak. We need to be so careful before choosing our words.

As you put toothpaste on your toothbrush each morning, say a little prayer asking God to guard your tongue and to prevent you from speaking negative words. Remember, you can't take them back! Be a blessing to others.

Dear pastor's wife, I ran across this scripture and it spoke to me concerning encouraging others. Isaiah 59:4 says, "The Lord God hath given me the tongue of the learned, that I should know how to speak a word in season to him that is weary: he wakeneth morning by morning, he wakeneth mine ear to hear as the learned."

We can pray every morning and ask God to give us the sensitivity to notice when someone needs an encouraging or refreshing word for them. People do get weary in their sorrows. Let us be that witness and ray of sunshine to them. Let's give them a word of encouragement.

Questions to Ponder

1. Were there times when I used my words in a careless manner that brought pain to someone else?
2. Think of someone that you can encourage and to bring words of life to them.

Dear Lord, I repent of using my words in a careless or negative manner. Please help me to remember to use words of life, so that I can make a difference for you.

CHAPTER 2

WHISPERING SAINTS

Judy tiptoed down the hall after checking on the sleeping kids. Judy and Bill had three wonderful children which they knew were a blessing from God. Church life could be demanding and frustrating for the children of ministry, but they seemed to have adapted well to being raised in a pastor's home.

Judy finished laying out the clothes for Sunday morning so there would be no confusion when it came time to get ready for Sunday school. She glanced at the clock, "9:30," she said. She decided since Bill was still studying at the church, she would have a little time to go through a few boxes of Christmas ornaments. She headed to the spare room which Bill jokingly named the junk room.

It was just about time for Thanksgiving to roll around and Judy was searching through the sealed boxes which had yet to be unpacked from their previous parsonage seven months earlier. Unpacking the boxes meant acknowledging that friends and relationships left behind were truly left behind. Each time she went through the boxes she was reminded of the friends she, Bill and the children had grown close to who now are travelling down a different road in life. For a little over nine years they had seen many blessings and made several life-long relationships. Ministry had its challenges but overall the people were supportive and the growth had been steady. It was hard to leave, but both Judy and Bill knew that God was calling them to a new field of service.

She thought to herself, "We'll get a chance to go back and visit them soon." But she knew in her heart that it may be a long while before that time would come. Judy realized the difficulty in making trusting relationships at a new church ministry, but it was even more difficult having to leave those relationships behind. That was just one of the many challenges in a call to the ministry.

People grow apart as their lives take new and different paths, when friends we leave behind have new experiences and challenges. We lose touch as we no longer share those daily times together. Our lives simply become short stories we recite to each other through letters and phone calls as we grow in different directions.

This is a unique experience in the lives of pastors and their families as they journey to a new town, city or state and try to plug their lives into the lives of members who grew up together, graduated together, raised children together, and have spent many of life's joys and sorrows together. At church fellowships and visits it often feels as though we are on the outside looking in as longtime friends and family reminisce about the good 'ole days.

Judy grabbed a box that was simply labeled "Christmas". Sitting on the living room floor she browsed through the box and caught a glimpse of one of her favorite collectibles. A dear friend had given it to her at their previous church. They had been there for about four months when Judy's mother had fallen gravely ill with a debilitating stroke.

Judy spent over a month back home helping her dad who had

some health concerns of his own, while her mother slowly recovered in the hospital. Eventually she had to return home to Bill and the kids. Living more than seven hundred miles away while Judy's mother had several ups and downs during recovery caused many anxious moments for her. To add to the anxiety were the adjustments to a new church with all the demands of ministry life, learning a new town and area. Then the basic challenges that come with everyday life took a great emotional toll on Judy.

She reached in the box and pulled the collectible up to eye level. It was a wall plaque shaped like a heart and was inscribed with the words, "Home is Where the Lord Sends You."

Judy's eyes began to mist over thinking of her sweet friendships that she had left behind. Then her thoughts drifted to her mother who was her best friend and went home to be with the Lord two months earlier. She tried to convince her father to move close to them and the grandchildren, but he wouldn't budge. He said he would never leave the home where he held her mom's hand as he handed her to Jesus for safe keeping until he could join her some sweet day. "So much has changed in a short time," she thought.

She stood up with the plaque in her hands and exclaimed out loud, "Well, it's time to call this place home and I know just where to hang this." She found the hammer and nail and headed off to the parsonage living room near the hall entrance to the garage. After hanging the plaque and straightening it into place, she stood back with a feeling of accomplishment and whispered a prayer, "Lord, thank you for our new home. Please bless it with peace, love and joy."

Just then she heard the car door close and Bill was coming through the garage door. She felt a sense of excitement well up within her as she thought, "For the first time I'm going to welcome him home and really mean it." She couldn't wait to reveal to him that she had come to terms with their new home and was willing to embrace the transition of the new life where God had sent them.

As he walked into the living room and removed his shoes, she smiled and said, "Welcome home." Her smile quickly shut down as she looked at his face and saw that he was visibly upset. Her mind raced as to what could be so upsetting to him.

Almost involuntarily she uttered, "What's wrong? Are you okay?"

Bill said nothing as he seemed to be choking back tears. Now she thought someone must have died so she walked over to him to place her arms around him and console him.

As she reached out to him she asked again with a sound of sympathy, "What's wrong?"

Bill embraced her and laid his head on hers and answered, "I don't know."

"You don't know? What's going on? Are you feeling okay?" she pressed.

"Honey, let's sit down. I need to share something with you. I have something to show you." Bill said gloomily. He didn't want to scare his wife, but he felt that she needed to be aware of what had happened.

Now Judy was scared and confused. Just three minutes ago she was experiencing peace and a newfound joy. She was content and happy and in a swift moment, she was sensing fear and gloom. Sometimes the ministry caused their emotions to change from one minute to the next.

"Lord, didn't you hear my prayer a moment ago?" she asked in her heart.

They both sat on the sofa and Bill pulled out a piece of paper from his shirt pocket. Judy could see a handwritten note, but couldn't make out what it said. Bill handed her the note and said, "I had a visitor at the church tonight."

She read the note and her heart ached. She could feel her chest tightening. She asked Bill, "Who was it?"

"I don't know," answered Bill. "They left before I could see who they were." He then proceeded to share his experiences of the night.

Judy began to cry silently as Bill held her. "What does this mean?" she asked. "How can this be? We can't leave. Our kids are just making new friends in school. I'm one of the 'Helping Mommies' in Jack's class. I just memorized our new bank account number and finally found a new dentist for the kids. Everything in our life that others take for granted is just getting stable."

Judy was pouring out obviously in pain over the note.

She jerked up and said, "You've got to tell Bro. Frank about this."

Bill responded, "How can I tell him? What if he's one of them?" It dawned on Bill that for the first time he realized that there was a fracture within the church. The uneasiness in the pit of his stomach confirmed even further that he didn't know who his friends were and who desired for him to leave.

Bill's thoughts began to race. "Did this include the deacons? Was Ms. Joanne part of the opposition? She was the church hostess and was the first member to greet us at the parsonage as we moved in. She had cake and homemade bread waiting for us along with a little basket of goodies for each of the kids. She was always super sweet to us and our children. But was this because she is genuinely sweet or does she have an ulterior motive?"

Bill wondered about Luke always making suggestions of people I need to visit that he has been to see. Is he trying to tell me I'm not performing to his expectations because I can't visit every member every week, or is he just being helpful?

Then there's Jill, the custodian who's always asking what Judy is doing that day. Is she checking up on the pastor's wife or is she just being cordial?" Suddenly everyone became suspect.

"Bill. BILL!" Judy stated adamantly. "Are you hearing me?"

Bill finally snapped out of it. He realized that he had not been listening to Judy as his mind raced. What had he missed? He was trying to remember anything that would give him a hint as to who the "we" were in the note.

"I'm sorry, Honey," Bill consolingly said. "I don't know what to think." He placed her hands in his as he drew her near and embraced her. He tried to be the strong, encouraging husband as he whispered in her ear that everything would be fine. "It has to be just a simple misunderstanding," he lovingly stated, but in his mind he felt a sense of fear and dread.

They prayed together and turned in for the night. Neither of them slept much as they tried to find the peace of God and His sustenance. After a fitful night they rose early, visibly exhausted, their minds working overtime, trying to make sense of what had happened the night before.

Bill arrived at the church earlier than usual that Sunday morning and headed for the sanctuary. He wanted to spend extra time in prayer seeking God for wisdom, but a bigger part of him wanted to make certain that there were no other surprises at the church before the members and visitors began to arrive.

One of the mysteries of a pastor's heart is that even when he is under siege, he has an inconceivable passion to protect the innocent among the flock from being scattered or harmed by wolves in sheep's clothing, even if it exposes him to assaults and being wounded. Many pastors have been picked apart and slaughtered while protecting the flock. Seeking to spare the flock from harm or divisiveness, they will take the abuse and internalize it as they seek God to intervene.

As he left the sanctuary, Bill didn't know what to expect, but what surprised him was an overwhelming sense of paranoia. As he greeted folks with a forced smile and a warm handshake, he couldn't help but try to discern the heart of each individual he greeted, wondering if they also agreed with the note he had received the night before.

As he walked toward the ladies' classroom, the chatter he could hear as he was coming down the hall suddenly ceased as he walked through the door. The atmosphere seemed to become filled with icy tension, rather than the usual cheerful greetings.

Bill's heart began to race as his adrenalin elevated and he could hear his heart beating in his ears. It was the same sound he had heard in the sanctuary the night before.

Ms. Suzan broke the chill with a hearty, "Well hey there, Preacher!"

"Uh. Good morning, Ms. Suzan. Um, how is Gary feeling today?" Bill tried to focus his thoughts on being the concerned pastor while veiling his suspicion at their odd behavior. It was unsettling to walk in on conversations that stop as he approached. He tried to concentrate on what Suzan was telling him.

"Oh, he's much better. In fact, he's here this morning," Suzan answered with a smile.

"So, what are you ladies talking about this morning? Or better yet, who are you talking about?" Bill chuckled and then added, "I'm just picking with you, ladies." He was actually hoping his question would reveal whether they were discussing him or if he was simply being overly paranoid.

The older ladies giggled and looked at each other, and then Shirley decided tell him what they had been discussing. "Before you walked up, we were discussing prayer requests and the situation with the Middletons.

"Yeah, we need to keep reaching out to them and praying for them. Greta is still in shock and the kids are trying to focus on their school work during this whole mess," Bill responded.

Greta's husband had left her and their three kids and since they were very active in the little church, it was being felt very deeply.

Many folks in the church were concerned.

"We were discussing how we could try to help her with Christmas this year, without prying into her life too much," Ms. Busby chimed in. "The only way to find out how we can help is to just ask her," she added.

Bill felt ashamed of himself for assuming that the ladies were gossiping about him, when they were simply discussing helping a family in the church. He felt ashamed that this family had a serious need for their pastor to be completely available to minister to them during their time of need. He needed to be available emotionally, mentally and spiritually.

When individuals launch an attack against a pastor, they don't realize that they are causing the church to become crippled. When the pastor or his wife are consumed with fears or emotionally damaged by accusations or assaults, they are like any other human in that they suffer heartache and emotional and mental anguish. But for the pastor and his wife they must suppress their pain in order to minister to the pain of others. No other calling in the world has such a mandate.

The church needs healthy and focused pastors, therefore the church must strive diligently to protect the hearts of their ministers so that they will be emotionally and mentally available and effective when they are called into action to meet the needs of their parishioners.

Bill listened to the ladies for a while longer, somewhat relieved that he had mistakenly assumed they were gossiping about him, which allowed him to relax a bit during their conversation. However, during their conversation his anxiety began to grow as his mind drifted back to the night before. As he headed toward his office, it dawned on him that he simply walked out of the classroom and didn't cordially dismiss himself. He hoped they didn't think he was being rude, but the thought of preaching with this difficult circumstance flooding his mind was now causing mild anxiety.

Even with Bill's seminary training, he was never taught how to deal with difficult church members and how to preach a powerful and encouraging sermon while pretending nothing is wrong when his whole ministry seems to be crashing down around him.

Walking down the halls, smiling and greeting folks, he couldn't help but feel as though he was a hypocrite. When folks would ask him how he was doing, he would issue the standard, "Just fine." Bill also tried to use discernment with each member, as to whether they were the culprit or whether they were a loving supporter of Bill and his wife. The myriad of emotions was taking a toll on Bill, and he could sense his blood pressure elevating as his mind was constantly racing.

He finally made it to his office and he settled in at his desk to go over his notes and pray. He decided to pray first and he could feel the tears welling up as he realized his heart was broken over this whole dilemma. Praying helped but since he had no answers as to what to do or what was even wrong at this point, he felt little relief. It was very insensitive of someone to leave a note like that the night before he was to preach. In fact, it seemed that the culprit didn't think he would see the note until he stepped up to the pulpit in front of the entire congregation. Would that person be in the audience this morning?

A person who does something like this has no actual concern for the mission of the church or for the people in the pews that need a healthy, united church to hear a word of hope, peace, encouragement or edification.

"How can I deliver a word from God with the weight of this realized circumstance brewing?" Bill thought to himself. "I'm just going to have to preach and block it out for an hour. Maybe I'll act super joyfully to throw them off track." He reasoned.

As he stood to open the Bible, his hands trembling slightly, he scanned the audience of just over one hundred attendees. He couldn't help but think that several faces could easily be the culprit. He noticed a family was not in their usual pew. They were nowhere to be seen. "I was sure I noticed them in the Sunday school building," he thought to himself. Then he noticed a few other regulars were missing. "How can I preach like this? Do they all know about the note?"

As he oscillated between thoughts he realized that he could not receive an answer and that at this point everyone was suspect he decided to press on.

"Please open your Bibles to the book of Romans, chapter 8 and verse 28..."

The next morning, Bill and Judy were sitting at the breakfast table. They were both exhausted from the busyness of Sunday activities and the lack of quality sleep.

Bill got up from the breakfast table and kissed Judy good bye and headed out the door towards the church. He was grateful that the church was just next door to the parsonage, except for the fact that many church folks who drove by during the day often assumed he was home watching television since he didn't have to drive to the church. He had thought about leaving his car parked at the church regularly just to throw off the nosy members.

As Bill went into the church and unlocked his office door, he fought back the urge to turn around and go home. Being at the church had lost its joy and excitement.

"Good morning, Dinah, how are you doing this morning?" asked Bill.

Dinah was the church secretary and had been working there for almost twenty years. She was a very cheery individual and was a perfect personality to be the first person anyone greeted in the church office. But as cheery as she often was, occasionally she could swing into extreme lows emotionally that could bring a stressful silence and coldness into the office.

"I'm doing great, Bro. Bill. "How are you?" she responded.

"I'm doing fine!" Bill knew he was not honest in how he was doing and felt a twinge of guilt at his answer. The Pastor is supposed to always be doing great and wonderful regardless of what he is enduring in his personal life, right?

He went into his office and sat down at his desk. He began praying under his breath for God to restore his joy and to give him wisdom. As he finished praying, there was a knock at his office door.

Definition of Gossip

Webster's Dictionary defines a gossip as a person who habitually reveals personal or sensational facts about others. If what we are about to say has nothing to do with us or our immediate family (people who live under your roof), then we have no right to share the information. Most of the time, if people wanted us or anyone else to know something, then they would share it with us themselves. It is not our place to share information about any other person. Over the years, I have heard people say that statements are not considered gossip if they were true. That is a <u>false</u> theory! Gossip can either be true or partially or completely fabricated. Simply, gossip is anything that is none of our business.

Gossip has become a multi-million dollar industry with magazines, news and television shows. And now the most popular gossip venues are social networks. People are anxious to hear about celebrities and what is going on in their private lives. Even though it may be interesting to some, it is really none of our business. Photographers earn large sums of cash preying on famous people in order to get that one photograph that will be the next big story. But it is at the expense of the celebrities and their families. Due to this sort of public gossip, they sometimes get depressed and even have to be reclusive in order to stay safe and to try and protect what little privacy they have.

The church is the one place where gossip should not be found, because people are supposed to be walking in the Spirit of God. We should be showing love and concern for others, not sharing other people's most intimate and private information. Gossiping is not something that is dealt with in most churches. People usually know who gossips within their church, but they overlook it and just expect it from them. We need to take a stand against gossip. We will discuss why it is necessary to take that stand and ways that we can do that in this and other chapters.

What does a gossip look like? How can you identity them? He or she looks just like you or me. They might mask themselves and be unnoticeable. They might hide behind a sweet countenance or a sugary sweet tone of voice, but the end results are still the same. People who gossip don't wear a big "G" on their sweaters so that we will all know who they are.

They may also be apparent or they may give themselves away with their body language if they are in the habit of gossiping. They sometimes have distinctive traits that are quite noticeable to the observant eye. They can be found whispering to someone with their hand cupped over their mouths often times looking or pointing at the object of their comments. Some people are blatant and they do not hide the fact that they are a gossip. Some are even proud of having that title.

Some of the more advanced gossips will actually ask lots of questions about people and are generally eager to share what they know about people, whether it is confidential or not. They may seem overly interested in other people's personal lives often asking others about a particular person's news rather than asking the person themselves. They may be genuinely concerned or they may feign concern.

Gossips generally gravitate to each other and form cliques that everyone else can see and typically fear. Some people will go so far as to avoid walking near them by taking alternate routes or waiting until they have cleared the scene. The cliques may or may not be intentionally formed, but they are obvious to others.

You can also identify what I call a "professional" gossip. They are such a pro because they have been doing it for so long. All someone has to do is simply walk up to them and say hello. The habitual gossip usually just starts discussing one topic after another and covers as many people as possible in a small amount of time. It is like watching an expert marksman taking out multiple targets with a rapid fire machine gun. It will make your head spin and if you have two of them, it is like watching a tennis match.

They are eager to share everything they know about an individual without any consideration as to whether it is true or not. In fact, truth is only as relevant as their opinion of what that truth might be.

You might not even have to contribute to the conversation at all. They are so caught up in what they are saying that they might not even notice if you comment or not. The danger of this one sided conversation is that the gossip walks away believing in their mind that you are in total agreement with their opinions. You have unwittingly added your name to their arsenal by simply being an observer of the onslaught. When they go to the firing range again with another victim they will gladly toss your name in the ring as a cohort and in some cases cause you to be the instigator of whatever gossip is prevalent at the moment.

I have walked up to ladies at church and greeted them and after a cordial hello, they would begin spewing negative gossip about people. Some of them go from one subject to another, while barely taking a breath. I wonder if they truly just do not realize what they are doing. There have been times when I simply just excused myself from a conversation.

Some gossips want you to agree with them or they ask you if you understand what they are talking about. I have said this more than once in this book, that it doesn't matter if the information is true or not, it is still not their place to share it. We need to be careful because just nodding our heads that we are listening might be interpreted to them as agreement or consent. I try to excuse myself and walk away quickly!

Someone seeing you talking with a known gossip might think that you are one also. When you walk away from them, just realize that they could be talking about you when you aren't around. It is a habit. Would the biggest gossip want those horrible things to be said about them? If the shoe were on the other foot, how would they feel?

This scripture comes to my mind: "Matthew 7:12 says, "Therefore all things whatsoever ye would that men should do to you, do ye even so to them: for this is the law and the prophets." The old adage of doing unto others what you would have them do unto you still holds true today. I am sure that you wouldn't want people to talk about you behind your back. So we need to be careful not to do that to others.

Gossip Affects Your Pastor's Family

Gossip affects everyone connected with the hurtful tales, including your pastor and his entire family. It is not uncommon to find that the pastor is the main course in Sunday afternoon dinners. Many families gather around the table after church and discuss the morning service. Their discussion might sound a little like this:

"The pastor sure was long winded today."

"I wonder who the preacher was talking about in his sermon this morning."

"Did you see what the pastor's wife was wearing today?"

"Those preacher's kids were rowdy in the morning service."

"That preacher was stepping on my toes today."

Or maybe it sounded like this...

"The preacher touched my heart with his sermon this morning."

"The preacher preached what God laid on his heart today."

No matter which direction those conversations go, it affects everyone at your dinner table, whether for good or for evil. We also fail to realize that children are listening to these same discussions. We are training them to carry the same practice and attitude into their adult lives.

I Peter 3:8 says, "For he that will love life, and see good days, let him refrain his tongue from evil, and his lips that they speak no guile". Our lives will be much happier if we use our tongues to speak love instead of hatred. Nothing good ever comes out of speaking negatively about people. If those comments ever get back to the person being discussed, it only brings pain to them.

The way we speak to people affects our workplace, our home life and people that we do business with. Gossip affects your friends, family and anyone that is the subject of evil words. Gossip affects everyone!

What Kind of Fruit Do You Produce?

Proverbs 15:4 says, "A wholesome tongue is a tree of life." I want to be a healthy tree of life, not a tree whose fruit rots before it is ever picked. Whenever I picture a tree of life, I see a vibrant, beautiful and healthy tree whose branches have leaves that blow in the wind.

I have seen dead trees that are very unattractive and their branches get so weak they break off at the slightest breeze that comes along. When all other trees are blooming and budding around them they stand starkly against the green backdrop as a shadow of death.

If the tree has a disease, it can become barren or produce unhealthy or rotten fruit. I have picked pears from the trees in our yard when I was a young girl and there were times when a pear looked perfectly good until I grabbed it to pull it off the tree. As soon as I grabbed hold my fingers would sink into the rotten fruit and it would be mushy and wasted. We don't want to be a mushy Christian. We need to live our lives in a way that will attract people to God and not chase them away.

We want to bring living fruit into others' lives, where it leaves a sweet savor on their tongue, like a ripe juicy apple or a fresh peach. We need to desire for others to want to be around us and not to avoid us when we come around. We can show God's love to others much easier if we are living it to the very core of our beings.

Fire

Let's compare gossip to a forest fire. We will see that there is a difference between an intentional fire and an unintentional one.

Fire spreads quickly and is very destructive. My husband is a volunteer fire fighter in our community and sometimes they get called out on some very serious fires. Not too long ago, the fire department responded to a huge grass and woods fire. Whenever the person called it in to 911 it was a fairly small fire, but by the time the surrounding fire departments responded to it, it had already spread over several acres. It took several fire departments working together and tag teaming to put out that fire.

The temperature was over 100 degrees that day, so after about four hours, another department came to relieve them. Instead of the fire shrinking, it just kept spreading like it had a life of its own, almost like it had its own destination and wouldn't stop until it reached it. It took several more hours to completely put out the fire and the fire fighters couldn't leave the scene until it was determined that it would not spark back up again. It started on the side of the road, possibly from a cigarette being thrown out of a vehicle window, and then it spread into the woods. The act of throwing the cigarette was probably not an intentional act and the person went on down the road not even knowing that grass and trees were on fire and that fire fighters had to risk their lives to put it out.

Gossip is like fire in that it does not have to be intentional to be hurtful. Some people carelessly toss words around about others and then they go on about their lives not knowing the damage that they had caused. Even though it might not be our intention to hurt someone, it still causes as much strife as if it were intentional and vengeful. The result is the same.

Even the Bible compares our tongues to a fire. It only takes one spark, or in this case one person, to start a whirl wind of gossip and controversy. Gossip spreads as quickly as a forest fire, and it kills and destroys.

The fire department was called out a few weeks ago for a woods fire that spread and burned down a house and arson was suspected. If it was arson, then it was started on purpose with the intention of it spreading to woods and houses. While it was in the woods, it wasn't as serious, but once it spread to the nearby houses, it became a very dangerous situation.

Once a story starts spreading, you cannot stop it because it takes on a life of its own. It can take off like a wild fire or a runaway train the moment you tell the first person. It is out of your control once the words are uttered. Even if you regret starting a rumor and wanted to change your mind, it may very well be too late.

James 3:5 says, "Even so the tongue is a little member and boasteth great things. Behold, how great a matter a little fire kindleth."

Kindling is small pieces of wood that start a great big fire. It starts with just a tiny spark. It is the same way with the tongue. A sharp word or short sentence can start a lot of great heartache and trouble for other people.

After my husband returned home from the fire, I noticed that he smelled very strongly of smoke, even though he was not near the fire anymore. He still had the stench and evidence of the fire on his clothes and the smell didn't go away until I washed them. Gossip leaves a stench on others in the nostrils of God. The stench travels from person to person as the tales are told. It can be cleansed by the Holy Spirit, through genuine repentance.

Saying one negative statement can plant damaging thoughts s in other people's minds about someone. Our words might influence others to change their feelings about an innocent friend or family member. James 3:6 says, "And the tongue is a fire, a world of iniquity; so is the tongue among our members, that it defileth the whole body, and setteth on fire the course of nature, and it is set on fire of hell." The tongue represents what is in the heart and if the heart is corrupt, it will affect the tongue and defile the entire body. When the tongue is not tamed, it originates from hell and it is our nature to be that way. A person cannot separate himself from his tongue, even though sometimes he wishes he could. It is a part of our body whether we like it or not. We will lead people away from God with forked tongues, instead of speaking things of God and leading them to salvation in Jesus.

I would never ask a gossip for advice. Neither would I confide in one, whether it is someone who is an intentional or unintentional gossip. They are not walking in the Spirit of God and they cannot speak the knowledge of God because they speak from "hear say" not from what "He says." The "He" is referring to the Holy Spirit.

The Bible says in Psalms 1:1, "Blessed is the man that walketh not in the counsel of the ungodly..." Always seek godly counsel no matter what. Make sure they have a personal relationship with God who prays and seeks Him. A habitual gossip will not generally keep your information confidential even if you ask them to. They are led by their habits to gossip. I have not personally met a true gossip who can keep a secret.

Prayer Requests

Asking for advice or prayer, solely with the intention of gossiping is irresponsible and it is usually done to soothe the conscience of the gossip. If we are asking for prayer, surely our intentions are honorable. I have found this to be true in some instances, but in others, it was only a vehicle to share what we know. This is not fair to the listener, who honestly thought you were coming to them for prayer.

Sunday school classes were not designed to be a place to gossip. They were designed for Bible study and public prayer. I can understand asking for prayer requests and actually praying for those people during the class. Classes are to be a support to one another, but there has to be a line drawn between praying and gossiping. Sunday school teachers have an enormous responsibility to be an example and to be encouraging to others.

At a prior church, people actually left their Sunday school class due to the amount of tale bearing and opinions given during the class time. There was very little time left for the lesson to be discussed. Eventually the class numbers dropped so low that the class was disbanded. People go to Sunday school in order to grow closer to God with a deeper study of the Bible.

How Do We Stop A Gossip?

How do we stop a gossip? Stop listening to them! Who has the power to stop a gossip? The answer is the listener. It's such a simple solution. Gossip can only survive if both components are active, the person gossiping and the person listening. Get rid of one and you have no gossip. If a gossip will not stop on his or her own, the listener has the power to stop it. The listener of gossip has a tremendous responsibility, whether to listen, and also whether to share the information with others, which can ultimately end in someone being hurt. Let's stop listening to gossip!

It doesn't matter if we believe the person who is gossiping. It is not our responsibility, as a listener, to share what we hear about others. Listening to gossip only encourages the person to keep sharing things with you. If a gossip has no listeners, then it will stop. There would be no point for them to gather information about others.

You can make a difference in your life and the lives of others around you by not spreading gossip and also by not listening to it. What if the responsibility of gossip spreading solely depended on you? What if the decision was on your shoulders alone? Would the gossip spread or lie dormant with you? Let's make the right decision to stop gossip in its tracks.

Pray

If you know someone who gossips, pray for the Holy Spirit to convict them of it and be an example to them. But more importantly, share Jesus with them and be bold enough to walk away, letting them know that you will not participate. Actions can speak louder than words. Jesus' interaction with others in the Bible is our best example.

Matthew 5:44 says, " But I say unto you, love your enemies, bless them that curse you, do good to them that hate you, and pray for them which despitefully use you, and persecute you." There are two difficult points for the Christian in this passage. First, we are told to speak well of those who curse you. Second, even though it may be difficult, we need to pray for the people who hurt us. Not the kind of prayer that asks God to "get 'em" but for God to bless them. We must strive to please God in this area and not to please ourselves or others.

If we spent more time praying for the lost people in our churches than gossiping about them, then our churches would be much healthier and more effective at reaching and ministering the way Jesus desires of us.

For a powerful Biblical teaching about praying effectively for the lost you can download a free copy of the book, [1]*Praying Effectively for the Lost* by Rev. Lee Thomas of Westlake, LA. You can find it at his ministry website: www.pelministries.org.

We have seen many individuals saved by praying according to the teachings he reveals and many other churches are experiencing the same results. You can order copies of the book in print form for free. They do not charge and simply operate and make them available through love offerings and donations.

Questions To Ponder

1. Have I participated in gossip or spread news that was none of my business?

2. What kind of fruit am I producing in my life? Vibrant fruit or diseased fruit?

3. Have I been guilty of listening to gossip that is none of my business?

Father, please forgive me for listening to and spreading gossip. Please remind me to speak words of wisdom and kindness about others.

CHAPTER 3

THE SPIRIT OF OFFENSE

Bill yelled, "Come in," as he quickly hung up the phone. The door eased open and in walked Frank.
"I'm not disturbing you, am I, Preacher?" asked Frank.
"No, not at all. Come on in." Bill got up to greet Frank.
Frank was a long time member and deacon whose family helped to start the church over a hundred and twenty years before. His grandfather was the first deacon to be ordained by the church. His father followed the same call as did Frank. They came from a long line of dairy farmers and did pretty well for themselves though living a simple lifestyle.
To the average person Frank appeared to be a plain man who may not have had much education. But to those who knew Frank knew better, he was a man who walked hand in hand with the Holy Spirit. There was a radiance about him and a calmness that seemed to make all your worries dissolve when he spoke to you. He enjoyed a good laugh but most of the time he was quiet and observant.

Frank was a thin framed man of average height. He was in his mid-eighties but seemed to have the energy of a teenager. He was a Purple Heart, WWII Veteran who had joined when he was sixteen by convincing them he was eighteen. He signed up the week after Pearl Harbor in an attempt to serve and defend his country.

He enjoyed doing all the little things around the church that others seemed to miss or overlook. No job was too humble or modest for Frank. He seemed to have a knack of fixing just about anything or knew someone who could.

As Frank sat down in the chair in front of Bill's desk Bill asked, "What brings you by the church this morning?"

Frank answered, "Well, I came by to invite you out for some coffee at the deli."

"Well, Frank, I've got a pot ready to brew down the hall…"

Frank stood up and said to Bill, "Grab your coat, Preacher. I'm driving and I'm buying."

Bill wondered if Frank even heard him, but instinctively he got up and grabbed his coat.

Bill buzzed Dinah, the church secretary, on the intercom, "I'll be back in a little while, Dinah. I'm going out with Bro. Frank. If anyone calls just tell them I'll call them back or they can call my cell if it's urgent."

"Okay, Preacher," replied Dinah.

Bill stopped at the door and muttered, "Hold on Frank, I need to call Judy and let her know I'm leaving for -"

"Don't bother," interrupted Frank. "Marge is over there to keep her company. In fact, she's probably already told her where we're going." Almost without thinking Bill followed Frank and got in the passenger's seat.

Marge was Frank's wife of fifty-seven years. She was incredibly sweet and never met a stranger. She always seemed to be in good spirits and ready to bless somebody with a compliment. She was always helping with the ladies ministries around the church but never seemed to push her opinions or advice. She knew how to bring the best out of others.

Frank and Marge made a wonderful couple together. It was evidenced also by the fact that even though their children were grown and moved away they each had wonderful families and served their churches in a variety of ways. Two of their three sons were active deacons and their daughter had married a missionary and spent many years in Asia. One of his sons is now running the family dairy business. Frank and Marge were highly respected within the church and the entire community.

After being seated at the deli, Frank broke the silence, "How are things going with you lately, preacher?"

Bill couldn't help but think that Frank was leading up to some unpleasant news.

"Everything is good, Bro. Frank...How about you?"

Frank sat quiet, staring at Bill with a gentle yet firm glare that caused Bill to feel uncomfortable. He was simply waiting for Bill to confess that something was indeed causing him concern.

It seemed that several minutes passed, even though it was only a few seconds. Finally Bill put down his coffee and conceded, "No, Frank, everything is not good."

"I knew something was wrong Bill. Let's talk about it."

Something about the way Frank approached the matter gave Bill a peace that he suddenly felt he could trust Frank with the details.

"How did you know, Frank?"

"I've been in the trenches myself, son. I know the look and smell of fear. Yesterday morning you looked as though you were waiting for a sniper to pull the trigger. You had no passion about the message you were preaching. You had a vacancy in your eyes at the end of the service."

"It's a good thing you don't play poker, Bill."

Bill hung his head for a few seconds while trying to hold back the tears. Through misty eyes he began to tell Frank all the details of the previous weekend. He pulled the note out of his shirt pocket that had been attached to the pulpit and handed it to Frank who listened intently, shaking his head in disbelief every now and then.

Finally Frank spoke up and admitted, "I didn't realize things had gotten so out of hand. I had hoped it would just die out. I've been praying for you, Bill, and for the folks involved."

"What about?"

"Well, Bill, do you remember when Ida Mae's husband, Jesse, fell and broke his shoulder?"

"Yes, I remember," Bill answered with a sigh. "It happened on a Friday and they took him in for surgery pretty quickly. I didn't find out that it even occurred until Sunday morning when someone mentioned it to me in passing. I was frustrated that nobody alerted me to his accident or surgery and that I couldn't be there to sit with her in the waiting room. Is she still upset because I wasn't there?"

"Yep! She still has it in her mind that you had to have heard about it and should have been there. She took it personally. But that is only part of the problem."

"Ida Mae passed her offense on to her daughter, Shirley, who then passed it on to her Sunday school class, and so on. Are you getting the picture, Bill?"

"Kind of. I couldn't have been there because there was no call or contact to tell me what had happened to Jesse. I know she has wanted Jesse to come to church with her for years and I wouldn't want to hinder him by any means. I even went and spent an hour with them at the hospital Sunday afternoon after church. We had a great conversation. For goodness sake, Frank, I was told in passing and as soon as church was over I went straight to see them."

"Bill, don't you realize that all pastors are supposed to have

ESP?" Frank asked.

Bill couldn't tell if Frank was being serious or if it was just his dry humor. Either way Bill was feeling disgusted with the entire situation. It seemed like he was living in a Twilight Zone moment. He couldn't be at a surgery for someone if he had absolutely no knowledge that something has happened. Now it was causing a major rift in the church.

"Bill that was simply a small seed of offense that she grabbed onto. That seed is now a full blown offense and is affecting others in the church. Unfortunately, we need to get some pruning done before God does. We must stop this before it spreads any further and does more damage."

"I don't know how things may turn out, but with a lot of prayer and humility we may be able to turn things around. But it won't happen overnight. Are you ready for a long journey?"

"I guess. But I don't even know where to begin," Bill dreaded.

"Let's begin with some prayer right now and then see what God shows us to do," consoled Frank.

With that they bowed their heads and Frank took Bill's hand and prayed an encouraging and eloquent prayer. Frank was a man of simple southern language but when he prayed it was as though he took on a whole new persona and he spoke with such grace and eloquence as though he were longtime friends with God Himself. Maybe that's because he was. Frank had a reputation of being a strong prayer warrior and now Bill saw it for himself.

"You finish up your coffee, Bill. I want to take you for a ride and show you something."

"What is that?" asked Bill as he wiped the mist from his eyes. Bill noticed that Frank's eyes were misty as well as he observed Frank pull a handkerchief from his trousers and dab his nose. It was at that moment that Bill recognized he had a true friend in Frank. He had had a comfortable feeling around Frank, but now he realized how true and genuine he really was. It warmed Bill's heart and encouraged him.

"You'll have to wait and see," Frank responded. The men stood up and headed for the door after paying the check.

Sharing Offenses

We need to be careful not to share in someone else's offense. It might not have anything to do with us, but the offended one could drag us into being offended just like they are. I have seen enemies become dear friends and form close bonds over the dislike of someone else. Some people couldn't even speak the name of another person, only their initials, and now they are friends because they teamed up against their pastor or his wife.

It is so sad that the rules are different in the mind of the critical church member than for the pastor and his wife. It is interesting that some groups of people can talk about the pastor and his family and they do not see it as gossip. (Later in chapter six I will expand upon this.)

They also keep secrets from the pastor, but not each other. The pastor or his wife usually doesn't have a clue that the person is offended until the family leaves the church and takes several people with them, and then it is usually too late to do anything about it.

The offense gets into the person's heart and if not resolved, could turn into anger, resentment and if left untreated, bitterness can settle in. Much of the congregation can know something that the pastor should know and they usually protect each other against the pastor, when he is the one affected by the offense. He is probably the only one who can actually repair the situation.

The spirit of offense has become increasingly prevalent in our local church bodies. Some people are waiting and watching for someone to say something so that they may feel offended and victimized. They wear their feelings on their sleeves, and get upset. Some are even comfortable in the role of a victim.

Many people have left their church because they were offended by the pastor, ministers in the church, or church members. What they do not realize is that when they are offended and then leave and go to another church, then they are taking that spirit of offense with them. This does not help them as a person and it sure doesn't help the church that they just left or the church to which they are moving.

Proverbs 18:19 says, "A brother offended is harder to be won than a strong city and their contentions are like the bars of a castle." Once a person is offended it is almost impossible to reconcile with them and then they become a prisoner to their anger. When someone gets mad, it is like a light switch is flipped off and they start looking at that person with critical eyes. Where they saw good things before, now they see the person's faults, and then they start nitpicking. They join forces with or gravitate to people who feel the same way, and it spreads as a cancer throughout the church and the community. Psalms 71:10 says, "For mine enemies speak against me; and they that lay wait for my soul take counsel together."

The solution to spreading offense is mentioned in Titus 1:11, which says, "Whose mouths must be stopped, who subvert whole houses, teaching things which they ought not, for filthy lucre's sake." Offenses can be spread with our mouths and can affect entire families and the Bible says that the mouths must be stopped.

It obviously was a problem back in Bible times or there wouldn't be scriptures about it. Maybe our generation can overcome this problem.

Attention

My husband was told that someone was offended because he didn't mention the Christmas decorations in the sanctuary. First of all, most of the decorations were behind the pulpit and he is generally facing the other direction while he is preaching. He and the music minister talked about it and the music minister commented on the decorations during the next service, but the offended people were not even at church that evening. So they continued to discuss the offense with others and even discussed it in the Sunday school class.

When a pastor gets up to preach, his mind is focused on God and on the message that he is about to deliver to the congregation. He has a serious responsibility to his flock and bringing them a message from God is as serious as it gets. The pastor doesn't need to be worried about someone being offended because their service to God was not mentioned. We need to have a spirit of humility when we do things around the church and there are times when people notice. Sometimes only God needs to know about it.

Jealousy

Jealousy is another reason people get offended. If a pastor mentions that he likes someone's cake or bread, then someone gets offended because he didn't mention theirs. The offended one had not taken the time to bring bread or cake to the pastor and his family, so he had no idea that they could make a cake just as good as the one who brought it to him. It is a shame not to be able to appreciate someone for doing a kind thing in public due to someone else's jealousy.

Blaming

Some people are offended and blame the wrong person for it. There was a Sunday school teacher who had taught her class for several years and it was known that she took off several weeks during the summer, and she usually got someone to teach her class. But instead, she told the youth minister so that he could find someone since he was the new Sunday School Director. Apparently, he didn't hear her and so he didn't get a teacher for the class. He wound up having to take his youth class and teach the younger class.

The next week, the youth minister called the teacher and told her that if she couldn't be there every Sunday that the church no longer needed her services. The pastor was not aware of the situation and he didn't know anything about the phone call until after hearing that the lady was offended and had already shared her offense with others.

The story that had gotten back to the pastor was that he had put the youth minister up to calling her. Funny thing is that they never considered the fact that while they blamed the pastor for initiating the call, they never considered the sharp and offensive tone of the youth minister.

The pastor called the lady to find out why she was upset and she told him what had happened on the phone. He told her that he was not aware of it and did not agree with the decision.

When the pastor spoke with the youth minister, he denied the conversation and stated that she became belligerent and resigned. The pastor offered to sit down with the two of them, but because she was so offended she left and never came back.

By the time the story got around, the pastor got the blame for the phone call and for the loss of a good Sunday school teacher, even though he had nothing to do with it.

Basically the youth minister did not take responsibility for his actions and allowed the pastor to become the target of offense from a situation that never should have occurred.

This is the result of a person being offended without resolving the issue. Instead, the teacher shared it with other people and left the church angry. The pastor didn't realize that he had gotten the blame until it was too late. She should have gone to the pastor to share her grievance if she didn't agree with the youth minister's phone call. At that point it could have been quickly resolved. There could have been correction with the youth minister and reconciliation for all concerned.

Forgive

This is a very difficult subject for me to write about because it is something that I struggle with from time to time. Tenth Avenue North has a song that ministers to me and also describes what I felt after I have been hurt by someone. The song is called, "Losing". I encourage you to listen to it. You can go to tenthavenuenorth.com to see the video. We do feel if we forgive, that we are the ones losing, but we can never go wrong in forgiving someone because God commands us to do just that. The song mentions that it is "wearing out my heart, the way they disregard." Being wounded by another person hurts down deep in our hearts, but the song goes on to pray for God to give us grace to forgive them. I find myself praying that.

The best scenario is for each party to forgive each other and love one another again as God instructs us. That is the best scenario, but isn't typically the way it goes. The following scriptures tell us very plainly and directly that we must forgive in order to be forgiven and to have an intimate relationship with Jesus.

Matthew 6:14 – 15 says "For if ye forgive men their trespasses, your heavenly Father will also forgive you: But if ye forgive not men their trespasses, neither will your Father forgive your trespasses." Matthew 11:25 says, "And when ye stand praying, forgive, if ye have ought against any: that your Father also which is in heaven may forgive you your trespasses." Before we even go to God with our requests or even to praise God, we must go and make things right with others. God is not obligated to act upon our prayers if we have unforgiveness in our hearts.

Do we have to forgive someone who keeps on hurting us over and over again? Matthew 18:21-22 says, "Then came Peter to him, and said, 'Lord, how oft shall my brother sin against me, and I forgive him? Till seven times?' Jesus saith unto him, 'I say not unto thee, until seven times: but, until seventy times seven.'" I know that this is a difficult thing to do, but if Jesus could forgive the ones who were trying to kill him, then how much more can we try to forgive someone who has offended us? Forgiving them doesn't mean that you have to be best friends with them. If you owe someone a thousand dollars and you cannot pay it back, so the person says that you do not owe it any more, that is forgiving you of the debt. This brings a sense of relief that you do not owe it any longer. The same is true with forgiveness, that person does not owe you any recompense for hurting you.

Luke 17:3-4 says, "Take heed to yourselves: If thy brother trespass against thee, rebuke him; and if he repent, forgive him. And if he trespass against thee seven times in a day, and seven times in a day turn again to thee, saying, I repent; thou shalt forgive him." WOW! I know this is hard to do, but if we want to have peace in our hearts, then we must do it.

Forgiveness is even a part of the Lord's Prayer. Matthew 6:12 says, "And forgive us our debts, as we forgive our debtors." In this prayer we are asking God to forgive us in the same manner and extent in which we forgive those who have hurt and betrayed us.

1 Kings 8:50 says, "And forgive thy people that have sinned against thee, and all their transgressions wherein they have transgressed against thee, and give them compassion before them who carried them captive, that they may have compassion on them."

One of the hardest things to do is to forgive someone who has hurt you so deeply, especially if it was intentional. We can be totally in the right and the other person can be completely in the wrong and we still have to forgive them. Sometimes we don't even get an apology and often they don't seem to feel remorse for what they have done to us. We don't know what it in their hearts. Sometimes pride or fear keeps us from apologizing.

We also must forgive people, even if they are dead. That is very difficult because there can be no restoration with that person. But we can confess our thoughts and feelings to God about the situation.

Another person whom we must forgive is ourselves. There are things that I regret in my life and I have made the wrong decision at times. There were times that I had wished that I could turn back the clock and go back and have a "redo". Looking back, I could kick myself for making some decisions, but I have learned that I must forgive myself for those mistakes. We must remember that God is forgiving, but we are not always so gracious with ourselves. In order to feel cleansed, we have to receive God's gift of forgiveness.

We must make sure that we don't harbor unforgiveness because we are not promised tomorrow and we may not get another chance to reconcile with that person. Regret and guilt are very heavy things to carry with us throughout our lives, especially if it could have been avoided.

Go To Them

This is not always possible, but Matthew 5:23-24 says, "Therefore if thou bring thy gift to the altar, and there rememberest that thy brother hath ought against thee. Leave there thy gift before the altar, and go thy way; first be reconciled to thy brother, and then come and offer thy gift." We need to go to them and make things right with others before we can truly surrender to God.

A dangerous thing about being offended is that many people who are upset with the pastor or his wife spread it around to family members or their friends instead of going to them directly to try and reconcile it. It is obvious when people gossip to others that they do not want to make things right with the offender. With today's technology, people can spread offenses much quicker than years earlier. Email, instant messaging and texting make spreading gossip much easier. A person can text several people before they even leave the church parking lot. And, don't forget the old fashioned telephone.

Typically, the offended one tries to get as many people as they can to share in the hurt feelings. The wisest thing for the listener of the offended is to tell the person to go to the one who offended them and try to talk to them and reconcile the relationship. Sometimes, just sitting down and talking things out will resolve the matter. Some people only want to be heard.

But if you go to someone with an offense and they do not listen to you, take someone with you to talk to them again. Matthew 18:16 says, " But if he will not hear thee, then take with thee one or two more, that in the mouth of two or three witnesses every word may be established." Take someone with you who can be completely objective if possible. You don't want to take someone with you with the intention of ganging up on the person or to prove your point in the situation. Reconciliation and restoring the relationship is the goal.

Intentionally Offensive

What if our pastor intentionally hurts our feelings? Sometimes a pastor can get angry and say something that he will regret later. We are to treat a pastor just as we would another brother or sister, privately seek to restore the relationship with love and kindness as I have mentioned in the previous paragraphs. Spreading a story without confronting the pastor causes problems and threatens the health of the entire church. Only if the pastor refuses to reconcile with the church members, should the problem be brought before others. We need to give our pastor a chance to explain and to apologize. We don't need to just assume what his reaction will be.

We need to be careful not to intentionally offend others. I knew an older lady who got very upset if someone sat in her pew on Sunday mornings. She said she had the perfect spot in the church for her, so that she would not have to turn her head at all in order to look at the preacher. One Sunday morning a family went to the church and sat in her pew while she was still in her Sunday school class. She walked up to the pew and told the lady and her children that they were sitting in her seat and she told her to get up out of her seat. The lady, who was a first time visitor, later told us that she did exactly what the lady told her to do. She got up out of her pew and promptly took her children and went back to her vehicle and left and never went to that church again.

We do not want to be the reason that someone stops going to church. You could be the difference between Heaven and Hell for someone. I know that sounds a little extreme, but it is very true. Every move we make is so important in dealing with people who need Jesus.

We need to realize that the community around our church is aware of what goes on inside of the church walls, especially if there is conflict. The reputation of our churches is very important in our communities. That starts with you and me as individuals and whom we can influence for good.

Questions To Ponder

1. Have I been offended by someone and shared that offense with others?
2. Is there someone that I need to forgive?
3. Have I offended someone, either intentionally or unintentionally?

Father, please reveal to me if I have offended someone and not been aware of it. Please give me the strength and love to forgive someone who offended me.

CHAPTER 4

SOWING SEEDS OF DISCORD

Frank and Bill pulled out of the deli and headed south through town. Bill began to wonder if he should call his wife and check on her.

"She's fine, brother," Frank stated as if he could read Bill's mind.

Bill just smiled and turned away to gaze out of the passenger window.

"So how far are we going?" Bill asked.

"Oh, just a few neighborhoods over that away," Frank responded as he pointed in two directions at once.

After another block, Bill began to get an uneasy feeling in the pit of his stomach. He was hoping that they weren't going where he was thinking.

As soon as they turned down Magnolia Street, Bill knew where they were going.

"Frank is taking me to Sam Carpenter's!" Bill thought to himself. Now his heart was sinking and his stomach was burning deep inside.

Sam was another deacon in the church. He made it clear to most that this was his church and things were going to be done his way. Sam would be considered a bully in the church. No one objected when he spoke and if they started to he would interrupt and force the issue. In the deacons' meetings he used the same abrasiveness and if he couldn't make it they would post pone the meetings.

Nobody seemed pleased with him but they always let him have his way. He had made it clear that the pastor was a hired employee and could be dismissed very easily. He also let Bill know that he was not his fan.

Frank could sense that Bill was getting anxious.

"Don't worry, Bill, we're not going inside. I just want you to see something. That's why I drove Marge's car, so maybe they won't recognize us."

Suddenly Bill felt his anxiety subside as he began to wonder how Frank could be so sly. Even more so, he couldn't understand why Frank was doing so much to both encourage and help him. He began to feel a genuine love for Frank, something of a paternal kind of love, like he was looking at his father.

Bill's father died at a young age, so that relationship was vacant in his life. Now it seemed that Frank was becoming a type of father figure to him. If any good was to come of this bizarre dilemma in the church, maybe it would be a great friendship with a wonderful man of God.

Frank parked just down the road from Sam's house where they could get a clear view.

"I want you to look at whose vehicles are there at Sam's house," Frank stated.

"Well, there's Bro. Jim's and that one looks like Bro. Randy's…"

"Correct! And who else's vehicle do you see?" Frank asked.

"Is that Bro. Larry's car, our youth minister?" Bill asked.

"Yes it is, Bill. He has been coming over here nearly every

Monday for several months now. He's not just coming here for the coffee."

"What's going on, Frank?"

"Well, it appears that you have a "staff" infection. How have things been between you and Bro. Larry?"

Bill was still trying to process his thoughts as well as the question just presented to him by Frank.

"I thought things have been cordial. Larry acts very open towards me at the office and when I'm around him," Bill responded.

He began searching his memory trying to discover any clues or hints that there might be a problem between him and Bro. Larry.

"What's going on Frank? Why are we here?"

"Well, Preacher, the short of it is this. Larry has been busy bending the ears of Sam and Randy as well as a few others. He has also been involved with misinformation and such with Dinah up at the church. And do you remember that misunderstanding with Jesse and Ida Mae?"

"Yeah! What about that?" Bill asked quizzically.

"Well, I'm sorry to inform you that Shirley called Larry when they rushed Jesse to the hospital and informed him of what was going on. She asked Larry to call you and let you know so you could meet them up at the hospital. I overheard Larry telling Sam that he forgot to call you and that he was concerned that you would get upset with him. Sam told him not to worry about it and that he would handle it."

"I was later told by my wife that Shirley mentioned during a ladies meeting that when she asked Larry if he had called you he told her he did call you and relayed the message. She then assumed you didn't care to be there for them when they needed you and Larry never corrected the situation. When you tried to explain to her that you didn't know about his surgery, she thought you were lying to her and there you go. The mess we're in."

All of a sudden, events of the past few months started to become very clear. There were things that Bill had noticed, but gave very little thought to. Such as Bro. Larry and Dinah looking uncomfortable when he walked in the office, especially if they weren't expecting him so soon.

Bill realized that they often stopped their discussions when he walked into Dinah's office at the church. He thought they were simply startled when he would walk in on them talking. Now he was beginning to get an uneasy feeling in his stomach again. He began to feel foolish like he had been deceived and taken advantage of.

Frank put the car in gear and began to drive off. Bill thought they were headed back to the church but it seemed that either Frank forgot the way back or had another destination in mind. The latter seemed to be on Frank's mind. At this point Bill felt he would be safer in the car with Frank than he would be in his own office. Going back to the office gave Bill an anxious feeling in the pit of his stomach.

"Preacher, when our last pastor resigned, he had been having some problems with Larry, some of which included disrespecting our preacher and getting these same deacons to intimidate him. After about a year and a half of stressful relations the pastor left and took another church in Tennessee. He was a good man and it was a shame what he endured. I, and a few others, tried to talk with them but when it began to escalate, our preacher chose not to be the reason for a church to split.

During the interim time Larry began campaigning to be considered the next pastor, even preaching as often as he was able. I began to see shades of his deception when he would preach and often belittle or correct the supply preachers or interim. He is very clever and most folks think he is just a nice inexperienced young man. But there is a remnant of those who can see the light, as they say.

We did consider him at one point but the search committee felt we needed someone new coming in who had experience as a pastor. It appears that Larry has not finished campaigning. I'm afraid you have an Absalom on your hands, preacher. There are a few of us folks who are aware of what he's done, but unfortunately he has infected plenty of people over the last few years and especially since you have been here. Funny thing is that even many of the youth are discontented with him. I had hoped he would have changed and settled down for the sake of the church."

"How could everything be such a mess, Frank? How could I have not seen all of this when we first came here?"

"Bro. Bill, a church is much like a couple wanting to get married. During the courtship they will put on their best, they will adore each other, and commit to all sorts of promises in order to complete the deal. But, once the honeymoon is over and everything settles down, everyday life sets in and it is not as much of a storybook romance. Do you get my drift, Preacher?"

"Yep! The honeymoon is over."

"Precisely now, I have a few questions for you."

"Sure, Frank. Anything." Bill was now completely bewildered, yet he felt trusting of Frank now.

"Do you believe that this is the church that God has called you to and still has a call on your heart to be here?"

"Absolutely, I am concerned for my family's welfare, but I know I heard from God. Judy and I both did."

"Do you love this church and are you willing to actively defend her even if it may be painful at times?"

"I do love the church and the community as well as my calling. I am not too happy with some folks, but I don't even know how many or who is involved."

Bill could sense a courage rising up within him as he examined his calling and commitment.

Yes, Frank! I am committed to our church. I am committed to God's call and I will lay my life down if need be for the sheep God has led me to shepherd."

"That's what I wanted to hear, Preacher. I knew I liked you when I first met you. The test of a true leader is not where he stands in the calm but where he stands in the storm."

Frank then reached for his cell phone and flipped it open. Bill quietly stared at Frank as he held the phone at arm's length to see the numbers to dial. Placing the phone to his ear, Bill could faintly make out the voice of a man on the other end.

"This is Frank," Frank abruptly said.

"We'll be pulling up in about two minutes. Do you have everything ready? Good. See you then." Frank closed his phone and looked at Bill with a wry smile.

Being offended can lead to sowing seeds of discord. One of the most disturbing things about misusing the tongue is when people sow seeds of discord among the brethren.

Proverbs 6:19 names sowing seeds of discord among the brethren as one of the things that God hates. "These six things doth the LORD hate: yea, seven are an abomination unto him: a proud look, a lying tongue, and hands that shed innocent blood, a heart that deviseth wicked imaginations, feet that be swift in running to mischief, a false witness that speaketh lies, and he that soweth discord among the brethren." A sweet friend of mine pointed out to me that in this scripture there is a list of "things" and "actions" that God hates. The interesting thing is that when sowing seeds of discord is mentioned, the Bible says that God hates "he" that soweth discord among the brethren. That is SO powerful that it opened my eyes to how serious this action is. I have had to recheck my actions to make sure that I do not sow discord.

We will study these different types of sowing ungodly seeds within the family of God. These habits cause so much strife and grief to a pastor and his family and to the church. If you say any negative statements about someone, to anyone it is sowing seeds of discord. This means even if you are speaking to just one person and you are being intentionally negative, that is still sowing seeds of discord.

The Latin definition for discord means "apart from the heart." It means to disagree and two people cannot have the same heart and disagree. God is very displeased with any discord, even within our families.

Some people make it their mission to go around and deliberately speak words of discord among church people and prospects. It has become their nature, as we will see in Proverbs 6:12-15. It says, "A naughty person, a wicked man, walketh with a froward mouth. He winketh with his eyes, he speaketh with his feet, he teacheth with his fingers; Frowardness is in his heart, he deviseth mischief continually; he soweth discord. Therefore shall his calamity come suddenly; suddenly shall he be broken without remedy."

This is a person who is continuously and intentionally sowing seeds of discord and it seems they do not have a conscience about it. It is such a habit that it controls their entire body and they sow, or cast forth, discord. They do not send forth love and comfort and they are not concerned with the feelings of their victims. They send out pain and anguish to the recipients of their sowing. But the Bible says that calamity will come suddenly to that type of person. They may not realize that they are reaping all of the seeds that they have sown into other people around them, but God knows.

One morning, a disgruntled deacon went to another deacon and asked how they were going to get rid of their preacher. The disgruntled deacon dropped dead that very night before he could set the ball in motion to remove the pastor from his position. The pastor didn't find out how the deacon felt until after he had died.

Sowing seeds of discord often begins with someone complaining and grumbling over a small thing. This happened in the Bible in 2 Samuel in the case of Absalom, who stood outside the gate to listen to complaints. The problem is that he didn't give a solution to the problem, but only added to the distress of the complainers, while turning the hearts of the people toward himself instead of the king.

Absalom woke up early and placed himself at the gate where men sit to see why people were going into the city. Elderly wise men would sit at the gate to give counsel directing people to where they needed to go. Businessmen would contract deals and direct visitors and others to do business with them.

Absalom was outside the gate to hear grievances from people and while listening to these people complain he would give false empathy to them making them believe that he was sympathetic. What he actually was doing intentionally was fueling their griping and planting ideas in their minds, undermining the king. He would indulge them by suggesting, "If I were king I would solve your problem."

By doing this he would undermine the trust of the people toward the king and deceive them that he would be a more benevolent leader for them.

There are individuals in churches that desire the people to follow their lead rather than the leadership ordained by God to the pastor. They secretly manipulate their hearts into believing that they have the best interest for the church over that of the pastor.

This happens in many of our churches. When the pastor arrives at his new church assignment, everyone is still under the ether of getting a new pastor and everyone is excited. But as time goes on and people get accustomed to the new pastor and things don't go their way, they start doing as Absalom did.

They start finding fault in him and spreading it to their friends and family members. As they spread this discontent to others, this undermines the pastor's ministry. It seems that people have lost respect for the position of the pastor, not the man himself, but his calling. Some people think they need to micromanage him and tell him how they want things done. Pray for him and ask God to show him what the Lord wants him to do. If God is in control, then it doesn't matter who gets their way. God's way is always best.

The fruits of division start by sowing seeds of discontent. We were at a church where a staff member and his wife were working against my husband. At first, we had a feeling that it was going on due to several strange coincidences. We found out later that they were not coincidences at all. The first week that this person came on staff, a discontented person filled his head full of negativity about my husband. That set the ball in motion because the youth minister was not experienced or in tune with God enough to realize that he was being used (although they were speaking against him when he was not in their presence).

When those people realized that this minister would go along with them, word of his discontent spread and from then on, if anyone had a problem with the pastor, they went to the disgruntled minister. There they received a willing participant against their pastor to the point that the staff member was then speaking maliciously against the pastor. My husband knew this was going on, but he was very patient with him, knowing that he was stabbing him in the back the entire time. When he went to speak to him about it, he denied it and blamed it on others. It was so disheartening. It turned the church upside down and the church suffered tremendously because of it.

Finally, my husband had a talk with him and told him that he knew he was not telling the truth and he finally confessed. Things seemed to have gotten a little better after that, but there was so much damage already done. In order to repair his damage, he would have had to go to all of those people on which he had influence and denounce the things he had said, but he chose not to do that, although he did make a public apology to the church. Some thought he was genuine and others didn't. Only he knows for sure. I truly hope that he later realized the damage he had done.

A sad fact about all of this is that he thought those people he was teaming up with were his friends, but they were spilling everything he said to anyone who would listen. What a shame! He eventually left the church to go to another ministry and it wasn't until then that people started sharing how deeply he had embedded himself into the church and how he had affected several families against the pastor.

Sneakiness

Asking questions can be a sneaky way of sowing seeds of discord or to encourage someone else to do so. For example, if someone walks up to another person and asks, "What do you think about that preacher?" "Has the preacher been to see you?" For one thing, calling him "that" preacher is a derogatory statement and lets the other person know how you feel before even going into detail. Asking that question openly invites people to speak against him and encourages others to see negative things about the person. This is dangerous behavior and God is not pleased with it.

Most people have an opinion, but they may not share it unless provoked to do so. You DO NOT have to answer those types of questions. Don't be bullied into it. You might think that they are your friend and you do not want to lose their friendship. You do not need friends like that. There are plenty of people around who will prove to be true friends and do not expect you to agree with them all of the time. You generally will find a whole group of people who will not agree with that person, but who just won't speak up. We need to pray for boldness and courage to be able to do the right thing.

Disruption

There was a young man in Pastor Wayne's congregation who said he felt the call to preach. Wayne spent time with the young minister, showing him how he formed his sermons and gave him tips on how to deliver a sermon. He also gave him opportunities to preach in the church, even though several of the church members did not approve of his letting him preach. They didn't care for his inexperience in preaching and said that they came to hear the pastor of the church. Pastor Wayne and Carol spent time with this family in their home and the kids spent time together and truly began to care about them as friends.

One Sunday morning, that young man stood up and announced that he and his family were leaving the church because of Bro. Wayne. Bro. Wayne was startled, but calmly asked the man what his charges were. He gave vague answers and then walked out. He had never come to Bro. Wayne to tell him that he was unhappy or upset with him. He had spent time with this man, showing him how to comprise a sermon. He had let him preach on several occasions, even though it was not a popular decision. This was a slap in the face because the pastor's family had also spent time getting to know his wife and trying to be an encouragement to her.

It came out later that the man had been influenced by a young minister and a deacon against Bro. Wayne. It was an immature move to make a public display instead of going to the pastor. The pastor cared for the couple and didn't see it coming, but unfortunately others knew that this man was going to disrupt the Sunday morning service and did not warn him.

Another minister on staff admitted later that he was aware that it was going to happen, but said nothing. Knowing that this man was upset, no one brought him to Bro. Wayne to try and resolve whatever the issues were. To this day, it has not come to light why the man got upset enough to slander him in front of the church. God definitely was not in those decisions and He would never guide someone to disrupt a service as that minister did. God is a God of peace and love, not of disruption and confusion.

This is definitely a case of someone sowing seeds of discord. He expected people to follow his lead against the pastor. It backfired on him because no one got up and followed him out of the church, like he had expected and apparently as they had planned. This young minister man lost a tremendous amount of respect from the godly people in the church.

We need to pray for the pastors and ministers in our churches. They need our prayer cover every day.

Reputation

What kind of personal reputation do you want? Sometimes you can recognize a wicked person by their speech. Usually what is in the heart of a person spills out of their mouths. They surround themselves with people who agree with them or people who put up with their constant negative opinions of others.

Psalms 52:2 says, "Thy tongue deviseth mischiefs; like a sharp razor, working deceitfully."

Psalms 52:4 says, "Thou lovest all devouring words, o thou deceitful tongue."

Psalm 10:7 says, "His mouth is full of cursing and deceit and fraud; under his tongue is mischief and vanity."

Proverbs 6:18 talks about feet that are swift in running to mischief. That verse doesn't say that people walk, it says that they are swift to run. Gossip and trouble excites them to take part in the mischievous behavior. Some people gravitate to trouble and they actually enjoy speaking about others. They will naturally choose friends who will enjoy being around that type of behavior, because Godly people will eventually realize what they are doing by the conviction of their conscience and would not want to be a part of it anymore.

I have known people like that and have had to pull away from that relationship. I don't want to be associated with that type of reputation. If you hang around with people who are constantly "stirring the pot" and they are not happy unless they are complaining about others, then people will assume that you have the same habits and reputation.

Sometimes when someone or a group of people are speaking against another, it gets back to them. Sometimes it opens their eyes to whom they can trust and whom they cannot. Just know that if you tell someone, even a church member, it generally doesn't just stay between the two of you. If it is negative, the infection spreads because that person has someone that they feel that they can trust, so they confide in them. Then that person has another person that they feel that they can trust and so on. When the dust settles, several trusting souls have spread the information all around the church and then eventually back to the pastor.

The Church Secretary

Maureen is a church secretary and she spreads deadly infection like a cancer. When a pastor came into the church that she didn't like, she started working behind the scenes against the pastor and became a spy for the deacons, rather than just getting to know the pastor and his family. She spoke against him and tried to make him look bad to people who came into the office or called. When she was spewing her poison, she assumed that her friends were keeping her thoughts and feelings a secret. That was not the case at all. In fact, some of them went directly to the pastor and told him what she was saying about him. After several people went to him with the same information, then the pastor was sure that this was going on.

Maureen is a church secretary who can spread dislike and antagonism toward a pastor like a deadly infection. When a new pastor begins his ministry he may have different habits and preferences that can rub her the wrong way. She has been the church secretary for many years and takes pride in training each new pastor how things will be done. She may allow her feelings and pride to cause her to work behind the scenes against the pastor and in some cases become a secret agent of discord by reporting to the deacons or board anything she feels is improper or to her disliking.

Rather than getting to know the pastor and his family and giving him the biblical honor due him, she will begin sharing her thoughts and feelings with close friends and associates, thinking that they will not repeat her words. That is rarely the case. Everyone knows someone who they can confide in with a deep, juicy secret and thus begins the spread of poison seeping into the fabric of the church community.

Maureen's attitude carried over to her deacon husband and that spilled over into the deacon meetings. Her husband would make decisions in the meetings according to the way she felt about it, not necessarily for the best interest of the church.

Maureen would tell people that she didn't care what the pastor thought and she would only go by what the deacons said. If the pastor tried to talk to her about something crucial, she would panic and call a deacon and ask them to go up to the church. She was guilty of spreading negativity about the pastor and she was afraid of being confronted about it. Because her attitude was so volatile, he didn't try to talk to her about it again and just simply relied on the other secretary in the office. She was an older lady who was a professional and even if she had an opinion about something, she discussed it with the pastor, instead of others.

Maureen teamed up with a minister in the church against the pastor and they swapped stories of their dislike of the pastor. Some of the instances were laced with lies and deception. The funny thing is that the minister was conning the secretary with his lies about the pastor and she thought that he was the one that she could trust. But he was speaking against her behind her back also, which is generally the case with gossips. The tension in the office was very thick, but the pastor kept on doing his job even though he was criticized on every turn. It was hard for him to walk into that office every morning and he was relieved when he was called to the hospital for a visit.

The person who answers the church phone is a vital part of a pastor's ministry. It can make or break him with the others in the church. When people would call in, even if she knew that he was at the hospital or visiting with someone, she would tell them that he wasn't there or that she hadn't seen him that day instead of letting them know that he was out doing his job. The person would call the pastor and ask him where he was and they would be surprised when he told him that he had let the secretary know where he was. She was deliberately sabotaging his ministry and undermining him as a pastor. Even if she didn't care for him, she should have respected his position. The pastor would give a task to the secretary and she would call a deacon first to get permission to do it and if the deacon didn't agree with it, then she just wouldn't do it. She was very rebellious and was the cause of a lot of dissention in the church.

The deceptive thing about her is that she was stabbing him in the back with a sweet smile and sugary tone of voice. People were deceived by her personality. The pastor even heard things with his own ears that she was saying and started praying for her. One of the sad things about the situation was that she could have gotten to know the pastor and his family, but she alienated them, even though her husband was a deacon. Her husband was also rebellious against the pastor. But eventually God delivered the pastor from that situation by moving him to another ministry.

Talebearers

Tale bearing is another form of gossip which hurts others. It is the kind of gossip which ruins reputations, reignites quarrels and leaves friendships in ruins. It brings terrible pain to its victims, who are hurt and angry and isolated from the church and community. The careless words of a talebearer hurt very deeply and they cause wounds in that person. Let's see what the Bible has to say about them:

Proverbs 20:19: "He that goeth about as a talebearer revealeth secrets: therefore meddle not with him that flattereth with his lips." Talebearers cannot usually keep secrets and the Bible says not to have company with them. Do not encourage the habits of a talebearer. If you are associated with them then others will think that you are a talebearer also. Once you are labeled a talebearer, then you could lose trust among your peers and will not have much credibility either.

Proverbs 26:20: "Where no wood is, there the fire goeth out: so where there is no talebearer, the strife ceaseth." This scripture is self-explanatory. If no one is spreading things about others that is none of their business, then there will be no more strife. Most strife is fueled by the tongues of the people who make it their business to spread gossip about others. All it is doing is spreading pain. Proverbs 26: 2:1 "As coals are to burning coals, and wood to fire; so is a contentious man to kindle strife." We now have social media for people to bear tales.

Proverbs 26:22: "The words of a talebearer are as wounds, and they go down into the innermost parts of the belly." This means that the words of a talebearer wounds others very deeply and we as Christians need to be there to help those that are hurting. We see the responsibility of the listener again. No listeners, no gossip.

Busybodies

One of my favorite shows on television when I was a child was Little House on the Prairie. One of the most memorable characters on that show was Mrs. Olson, who was a busybody. I remember the episode where she got her husband to get telephones installed so that she could listen to other people's phone conversations.

Another busybody on television was Cora Beth on *The Waltons*. She made everything her business, including mail that came in for people, telegrams and phone calls.

I remember a particular episode where she received a telegram for the Walton family and she rushed it over to them and then they politely dismissed her so that they could read it. She was so disappointed that they didn't read it in front of her because she was dying to know what was in that telegram.

[3]Strong's Concordance defines a busybody as one who is overseeing others' affairs, i.e. a meddler. They meddle in other folks' affairs. So they are going around being nosy about other people's lives.

²Zhodiates Complete Word Study Bible says that busybodies are people who scurry about fussing over and meddling in other people's affairs, being overwrought with unnecessary care. If you want to know what is going on in the neighborhood, ask a busybody.

2 Thessalonians 3:11 says, "For we hear that there are some which walk among you disorderly, working not at all, but are busybodies."

1Timothy 5:13 says, "And withal they learn to be idle, wandering about from house to house; and not only idle, but tattlers also and busybodies, speaking things which they ought not." This scripture tells me that they not only seek out information about others, but they aggressively seek out people to tattle it to. They are idle except for the job of being a busybody.

Sally was a 65 year old woman in the church who, back in her younger prime would work with the preschoolers and teach in Vacation Bible School. Instead of putting her energies toward ministry, she now used them to criticize the people who were now filling those positions. She spoke about things that she had no business even knowing, let alone sharing it with others. Whether she did it intentionally or not is unknown. The hurt and anguish she caused was the same. That is one reason that bored and idle hands are very dangerous.

Liars

Lying is another way to create and spread discord among the church and community. Let's take a look at what the Bible says about liars and the act of lying. These scriptures are self-explanatory.

Proverbs 12:22 says, "Lying lips are abomination to the LORD: but they that deal truly are His delight."

Proverbs 13:5: "A righteous man hateth lying: but a wicked man is loathsome, and cometh to shame."

Psalms 31:18: "Let the lying lips be put to silence; which speak grievous things proudly and contemptuously against the righteous."

Proverbs 26:28: "A lying tongue hateth those that are afflicted by it; and a flattering mouth worketh ruin."

Jonah 2:8: They that observe lying vanities forsake their own mercy.

Matthew 5:11: Blessed are ye, when men shall revile you, and persecute you, and shall say all manner of evil against you falsely, for my sake.

Ephesians 4:25: Wherefore putting away lying, speak every man truth with his neighbour: for we are members one of another.

Jeremiah 9:5: "And they will deceive everyone his neighbor, and will not speak the truth; they have taught their tongues to speak lies and weary themselves to commit iniquity."

As you can see in these scriptures, God is not pleased with people who lie, and the Lord is delighted with people who tell the truth. This can lead to a very lonely existence. No one probably likes to be known as a consistent liar, but those people do exist inside and outside of our churches. Once a person has a reputation of lying, then it is wise to not believe anything they have to say. Lying breaks down the trust between people, whether it is between friends, family or church relationships. That person would have to spend time building up the trust of others around them. So much unnecessary work and wasted time is spent having to redeem yourself in the eyes of others.

Again, the remedy for sowing seeds of discord is to keep our discontent to ourselves and not to listen to others who are sowing seeds of discord. If we mind our own business and not talk about others, then we will not be guilty of hurting our church friends and family.

We need to pray for those around us who sow seeds of discord in any form and be an example to them by not listening and walking away.

Questions To Ponder

1. Have I sowed seeds of discord among my friends or in my church?
2. Have I been a talebearer or a busybody?

Father, please forgive me for sowing seeds of discord among my church friends or in my family. Please remind me to mind my business and to love others.

Chapter 5

UNDER THE INFLUENCE

    The two men pulled into a modest yet lovely home that had a well manicured lawn. Bill knew this home. He had been here several times before. This is where Bro. Henry Jacobs lives. Henry is another deacon and happens to also be the treasurer for the church.

    The driveway was quite long and disappeared behind the house out of view. The yard was occupied by many pine trees making the house somewhat difficult to see from the road. They pulled up the drive and around to the back of the house where Frank stopped and turned off the ignition. Opening the door, he motioned to Bill and said, "Let's go inside, Preacher."

    Bill stepped out of the car and began to stretch, realizing they had been sitting for almost an hour.

    "I need to call and check on Judy," Bill said as he pulled out his cell phone.

    "Okay, Preacher, but don't be too long. We need to get this done quickly," Frank responded.

Now Bill was again puzzled. He was puzzled enough to keep his call to his wife very brief. She sounded like she was in a good mood so he assumed her visit must have been going as well as his.

Bill couldn't help but smile as he thought about how mysterious Frank had been acting all morning. He felt as though he were working alongside a secret spy. Bill was in for a surprise.

"We're in here!" Frank shouted from the home office of Henry.

"Hey Preacher! How are you doing?" Henry greeted Bill as he walked in the office.

"I'm fine," Bill responded. "How's Lucille?" Bill asked.

"Oh she's out spending all my money." Henry laughed out loud.

Henry is a loud talker with a happy disposition. He is a typical treasurer. He takes care of the church's money as though it was his own, but he is always supportive of new ideas, especially if they involve reaching out to the children and young people. He truly had a heart to minister.

What Bill didn't know about was Henry's background. Henry was a secret agent during the Vietnam War before it was officially a war. He spent a year and a half as a prisoner of war in Vietnam before escaping miraculously. Henry and all of his fellow prisoners had been assembled and executed with rapid machine gun fire. Henry was the only one to survive as he pretended to be dead, but he was only wounded in the leg and arm.

He later worked as a Secret Service agent under President Ford until he took a job as a Federal Forensics Detective. He retired and was sometimes called back for consulting or when there was a major crime where they needed his expertise.

Henry is also one of the most honest men in the church with an incredible grasp of the Bible. Some say he has a photographic memory. Others say he is a genius. Either way, he has a humble, lovable way about him. Bill always thought of Winnie the Pooh when he was around Henry, but then he would rebuke his thoughts when they popped into his mind.

"Sit down over here, Preacher," Henry motioned. "Now be real quiet and let's see if we can get this to work."

Bill obliged as he sat on a comfortable leather sofa. He looked over at Frank and Henry as they both sat at the desk and Henry pressed the speakerphone button on his desk phone. Bill could hear the dial tone and then Henry dialing some numbers.

Bill was totally in the dark as to what they were doing there. Frank looked over at Bill and put his index finger over his lips gesturing for Bill to be silent.

The phone rang twice and then a cheerful voice answered, "Cornerstone Community Church. How can I help you today?"

"Hey! That's our church he's calling. What is he doing?" Bill thought to himself.

"Well, hello there, Ms. Dinah. How are you doing today?" chimed Henry.

"Well hello Bro. Henry. I am just fine. How is Lucille this morning?" she chimed back.

"Oh, she left with my credit card to go shopping with her sister. She should be back in a couple of days if I'm lucky." Henry guffawed out loud.

"Listen Dinah, can I speak with Pastor Bill for a minute?"

"Well I'd love to transfer you but he hasn't been around today," Dinah responded. Her tone was now sounding a bit agitated.

Bill sat forward quickly and Frank motioned for him to sit still and just listen.

"Oh, do you know where he might be?" Henry asked again.

"Well, I really don't. He's probably out playing golf somewhere or who knows. I gave up trying to keep up with him a long time ago," Dinah answered with a fake laughter.

"Well, is he in the office on Mondays? Did he leave a note or anything?" Henry questioned. Henry was known for asking many and unusual questions, probably due to his line of work.

"Sometimes he is and sometimes he isn't. You know it would make my job a lot easier if he would keep me informed. I just can't work like this. I think he enjoys golf more than he does being in the office where people can find him when they need him.

You know, you didn't hear this from me, but there are a lot of people coming to me complaining about Bro. Bill. I've tried to stay out of it but it's just eating me up," Dinah pleaded.

Henry in his usual fashion did not offer any criticism. He was a man who thought things out before he answered or gave up any information.

"Well, Dinah, I'll have to look into that."

Frank interrupted Henry by sliding a small note pad over to him on which he had written something. Henry nodded then proceeded.

"How about Bro. Larry, is he available?" Henry asked.

"Well he was but he has someone in his office right now and can't be disturbed. Someone came in and said that they had an appointment with Bro. Bill, but since he didn't show up Bro. Larry offered to help them out, just, uh, you know, till Bro. Bill makes it in or whatever.

I'll tell you now, that Bro. Larry he is a hard worker. I sometimes wonder if we should have hired him to be the pastor." Dinah chuckled trying to laugh off the insinuation.

"But I better keep my mouth shut before I get into trouble." She chuckled again.

"Okay, Dinah. If you wouldn't mind please leave a note on Bro. Bill's desk and have him call me as soon as possible. It's not an emergency, but I do need him to call me back soon."

"I sure will, Bro. Henry," She assured him.

They hung up and Henry turned to Bill and said, "Now when you get to the office I want you to find that message and call me."

"Okay," Bill said slowly and with a puzzled look.

Bill was beside himself as he stood up and started pacing. "I didn't have an appointment today! And Larry isn't in the office. He's over at Sam's. She outright lied." Bill was getting angry. "What is going on here? Just last week I thought everything was fine and then all of a sudden some mystery person is plunging a knife in the pulpit. Now I am wondering if my family might be in danger, not to mention our income, the home we live in, our ministry we have invested in, in this town, everything. I just don't…"

"Calm down, Preacher." Frank stood and went over to Bill to relax him. "You are not alone in this thing."

"Sit down, Bro. Bill, and we'll fill you in on what's going on." Henry spouted. "Would you like some coffee or tea?"

"Sure, brother, some coffee will be fine," Bill responded.

"Great. You wait here and I'll be back in a bit. I made a pot before you two got here," Henry said.

When Henry got back, they sat at a small round table in Henry's office. Frank began filling in Bro. Bill about what has been going on and why they had just made the phone call the way they did.

"Did I hear you correctly, something about a knife in the pulpit, Bill?" asked Henry.

"I'll bring you up to speed later Henry," stated Frank.

"Basically, Preacher, the last pastor we had shared some complaints about the church secretary giving misinformation about his whereabouts. We began to investigate and discovered it was true, but by that time things had become too unraveled and our pastor decided to resign.

When he would be out of the office and someone would call to speak with him the secretary would be vague as to his absence or presence in the office. On a few occasions, he was in the office but she led folks to believe he had not come in. This in turn would upset folks into believing that he was not showing up or doing his duties as pastor."

"Well, couldn't the Personnel Committee talk with her and maybe reprimand her?" Bill asked.

"We tried." responded Henry. "But she denied doing any such things and turned the criticism around against the pastor. After the meeting, several committee members were convinced that the pastor was the problem and some of us knew the truth while others were undecided. What makes things worse is that she is kin to several families within the church."

Frank picked up the discussion, "We did nothing more except for a few of us praying for her and the others being divisive. The pastor left and we had hoped that with a new pastor everything would be different. But, as we have recently discovered, they're not. Sometimes things need to be restored before bringing in a new pastor. Oh well, hindsight is 20/20 as they say."

Preacher, a secretary can make a pastor's job easier or more difficult. We didn't want to believe that this was going on in our church. We have some of the ladies and a few men in the church who are praying regularly about the situation and we also realize that if we are going to see our church become healthy and effective in the community we are going to have to become more involved and engaging."

"Look, I don't want to be the cause of any dissension or spilt in the church," interrupted Bill.

"Well, Preacher," chimed Frank. "If you will pray with us, keep preaching the Word to us and give us some time, I have confidence in God that He will give us wisdom and guidance and remove the spirits that are working against His church."

"It was Jesus who said that the gates of hell will not prevail against His church," Henry stated with confidence.

"Preacher, we have tried subtle conversations. We have tried to be patient and give these folks time to repent and since we see this will be a continual pattern of disruption and division, then it is time we begin to stand up for Christ by standing up for our church," Henry continued.

"So where do we begin, Bro. Frank?" asked Bill. "Whatever we attempt I want to be certain we seek for a conclusion of restoration and reconciliation if at all possible."

"I would love nothing more Bill, but the unfortunate reality is that sometimes these things do not end well so I suggest we begin right here, right now with fervent prayer," answered Frank.

They each took a turn praying. In the midst of praying, Bill could sense the presence of God and an overwhelming peace that he had not felt for a long time especially since Saturday night.

"Secondly, Preacher, we begin by committing to you our love and our support to walk alongside you as our shepherd. I want you to know this, Preacher, those who are stirring and nit picking are just a handful of individuals. But they influence a number of members through either relationship of using deceptive tactics of misinformation or even fear. They give the appearance that they are in the majority of opinion, but they are only leading the sheep astray."

"You know, Bro. Bill," Frank continued, "the Bible speaks of wolves in sheep's clothing in Matthew 7:15-17. It begins by giving a warning against 'false prophets'.

Many people try to associate that passage with preachers and pastors, but the truth of the matter is that the term 'false prophet' is also translated as a 'religious imposter'. That means that anyone can be a religious imposter whether they are a preacher or a typical church member. I also would like to mention that it speaks of the religious imposter posing as sheep, among the flock, not necessarily as shepherds leading the flock.

The Tongue: A Force of Life or Death

I do believe this is what we are dealing with here. We have a den of wolves, 'religious imposters', posing as sheep and are devouring our flock.

Preacher, you are the shepherd that the Lord has sent to us and the majority of the church will follow your leadership through this mess if you are following Jesus. If you will just minister to us, love us and preach the Word to us then some of us men and ladies will take care of most of the details to help turn this thing around. Are you committed to us? Will you pray and do what it takes to stand up against the wolves and protect the flock?"

Bill looked down for a moment and then looked at Frank and stated with boldness, "Absolutely, Frank!" He then looked at Henry and gave the same affirmation.

"Amen, brother!" exclaimed Henry.

"Okay!" stated Frank. "Here's what we're going to do first.

Negative influences have a domino effect. A youth minister, named Ricky, went to a church in a small town. A few days after he arrived, Deacon Tommy, who didn't care for the pastor, vented negative things to Ricky. Due to Tommy's influence upon him, the youth minister never gave Pastor Anthony a chance to get to know him or to even work with him. Since that time, the minister worked around the pastor and left him in the dark many times during his ministry. Deacon Tommy was not being a good example to the young minister and that set a pattern of disrespect for the pastor. Tommy infected others in the deacon body and that made life very difficult for Pastor Anthony and his wife. He would be sarcastic in deacon meetings; nitpicked his sermons and was even seen laughing and making fun of the pastor while he was preaching.

Bro. Ricky also spread his negative opinion of the pastor to anyone who would listen to him and he became friends with people whom he influenced to feel the same way. Some of the people didn't feel that way until his continued influence. So in essence, the negativity started with a deacon, which spread to the youth minister, which then spread to several people whom Ricky influenced.

Pastor Anthony's wife was beginning to have a good relationship with several people and when they became friends with Ricky or his wife, they started pulling away from the pastor and his wife. That was a good indication that attitudes were being spread. The pastor's wife even went to the deacon to try and reach out to him and she felt like things would be smoother with this person, but they weren't. He asked questions about her husband and seemed to understand the answers to his questions, but his pattern of nitpicking had become too much a part of him and he didn't change it. Proverbs 23:9 says, "Speak not in the ears of a fool: for he will despise the wisdom of thy words." A person is foolish if they don't want to hear wise words and to make things right with their brother or sister in Christ.

The sad part is most of the information that he shared was not even accurate. For several years those men attacked the pastor instead of working with him. When Pastor Anthony had had enough, he decided to resign. The last Sunday that Anthony was there, the deacon apologized to Pastor Anthony saying he was sorry that he made his life difficult. It was disappointing that this person didn't take a stand and do the right thing when it counted. Instead, he soothed his own conscience by apologizing as the pastor was leaving the church.

The pastor graciously accepted his apology, with extreme sadness. If that deacon would have done the right thing in the first place, then the years would not have been difficult and the minister (whom he had influenced) would have worked with the pastor as he should have. That apology tells me that he knew that he was making life hard for him and didn't heed the Holy Spirit's tugging to make it right.

There was a small group of people who sat together in church and they would heckle, cough, and speak sentences aloud at my husband while he was preaching. They would make noises and laugh and say negative things about him while he was in the pulpit. There were people who came to visit our church and they sat in that area, and mentioned later that it was going on. They were not interested in coming back because of that. Unfortunately, they were not the only visitors who had that same experience and never stepped foot in the church again. Visitors usually sit in the back of the church and that is where these people were. There were also a couple of people who would pick his sermons apart and judge every word that came out of his mouth. As they are sitting in judgment, they might want to study the verses and sermon ideas before criticizing. It also distracts the pastor and he loses his train of thought.

I know a couple who would take the sermon DVD home with them and pick apart every word. That is someone who is just looking for something against the pastor. Sometimes they would go to the pastor and tell him that he misspoke even one word. Preachers talk for a living and sometimes they will make a mistake and say things from the pulpit that they do not even realize.

Sometimes people would sit in the choir during the sermon and many times comments were made about the "show" that was going on in the choir behind the pastor while he was preaching. That is public disrespect and many church members were disappointed in them as they called themselves leaders in the church.

One of my friends is a pastor's wife and she told me about the disrespect that she received while she was trying to teach a ladies Bible study. As she was teaching, she saw two women who had seated themselves away from everyone else at the back of the room, putting their hands over their mouths, while talking and laughing. It disrupted her train of thought and also her confidence. This type of behavior makes the teacher think that she is the subject of the giggling. One of the ladies might have wanted to learn something from God during the study, but was influenced and distracted by her friend who was trying to be disrespectful. Be respectful to the preacher or the teacher as they are there to help you. They have spent time studying to be prepared to teach you what God has laid upon their hearts.

There was a rebellious older lady who refused to close her eyes during invitation just because the pastor said to. She sat there with her eyes wide open, thinking that it would affect him, but he knew she was being rebellious and that was not pleasing to God, so he just ignored her and went on with the invitation each time. Silently he and I prayed for her during that time, but her heart was so hardened that she wouldn't let God deal with her on her feelings about the pastor.

One Sunday, he made a statement about keeping your eyes open and being in rebellion and he looked right at her. That was the only time that she actually closed her eyes during invitation time. Her attitude didn't stop God from moving within the church body. If she only knew that she was wasting her energy making sure to keep her eyes open. She was trying to influence the pastor to be distracted during the invitation, but the pastor was focused on reaching people.

We need to not let anyone or anything influence our opinions and actions. We should develop our own opinions and thoughts about people and life in general. As a child and young lady, I was so shy and I wanted people to like me so much that I rarely gave my own opinion. I would listen to what their opinion was before stating my own, so that I would be liked and get approval. Have your own opinion about things and do not conform to others, just to be liked. If you start a relationship with that pattern, then it will carry on as the friendship grows and you will lose your identity.

I was scared of people for most of my life and it took me many years to get over that and just be myself. God has given me courage in dealing with people. I learned how to have healthy relationships, as I didn't have a clue when I was a young lady. I made so many mistakes and if I could turn back the clock with the knowledge that I have learned throughout the years, I would do things very differently.

I have learned that I don't need other people's approval just to feel confident and that my neediness was smothering. I have found my confidence in my identity in Jesus Christ. Not in other people's opinion of me. My energy is expended to please Him and seek His approval with my decisions and actions.

Unhealthy Influence

Television can influence us also. When I was a child, as young as 7 or 8 years old, I was addicted to watching soap operas. Back then, we didn't have all of the television channels that we have now. There were not many choices, although that is no excuse for my getting hooked on them. I watched them throughout my teen years and into my adult years. When I was in high school, I watched them throughout the holidays and if someone was sick from school, I would call them to see what had happened on the show that day. As a child, every lady I knew watched them and they would even get together at each other's homes and watch them together. When I worked, I made sure to take my lunch break during one of them. One holiday week would bring me up to date on several months of shows.

To tell you how hooked I was, in later years while I was at work, I would tape three hours of soaps every day and then spend the evening watching them every night. I remember being upset if the recorder didn't tape them that day. Later, when I was not working outside of the home, I would plan my appointments around those hours, so that I wouldn't miss them. Looking back, I am saddened by all of the wasted time. We didn't have children then, so that was my life. I was married for several years before I realized how addicted I was.

When I was a young lady, I made some terrible relationship mistakes, due to their influence. I was so involved with those shows I thought that was the way relationships worked, leading me to make some irresponsible decisions. Those were decisions that I would live to regret. I saw what appeared to be a glamorous and exciting life. I wanted to be like those women and I got so caught up in their lives. Some of my friends would even get depressed about the sad things that happened on those shows.

I found that if we are influenced long enough by something, then our minds will become trained and will think that this is normal. Since I started watching those shows at such a young age, it became a habit and it influenced me in a very negative way.

God convicted me of the dependence on the soaps and many years later, He delivered me from that bondage. I found out years later that I was not the only one who was addicted to those shows.

I knew a couple of deacons at a prior church, who were in their 80's, and when it came time for a certain soap opera to come on, they dropped whatever they were doing and went home to watch them.

When I was a teenager, there was a lady in our community who had to stop watching soap operas because she found herself seriously praying for the characters when they were in trouble. Another time, there was a group of ladies, including the pastor's wife, who were having a lengthy discussion about some of the characters in their favorite soap. The pastor walked into the living room and sat down listening intently as they explained the perils of a particular family. He was feeling sorry for the people and was thinking of what he could do to help when he found out that they were talking about soap opera characters.

People fall under their influence for one reason or another. We will look at some of those reasons.

Peer Pressure

Peer pressure is one reason to fall under the influence of someone who is habitually negative. It is easy to recall the feelings of peer pressure that we had when we were children and teenagers. Just because we are adults doesn't mean that we are immune to it, especially in churches. At times, we will listen to or spread information in order to please someone or to get their approval.

I know people who team up with the people who are keeping things stirred up. They swing from one set of friends to the other due to peer pressure. Be careful, because once you start that pattern with someone, they will come to you to see what you know about people. That is not a genuine relationship. That is a conditional relationship that exists as long as they are getting information.

Some people pressure others to work against the pastor or his wife. Sometimes it just seems easier or popular to go along with them. That influence can disrupt an entire congregation. Committee members also influence others, often before a meeting. Committee and business meetings are the place to state your true opinion about things not on the phone with your friends. It is not right to keep silent in the business meeting if you are going to get on the phone when you get home and call your friends and give that opinion. All of a sudden, all of your friends feel the same way that you do and that creeps into the morale of the church.

Some people will wait to speak their opinion only after they have campaigned enough to get a group to back them up. I wonder how many campaigners prayed for God's will before hopping on the phone. Churches would have fewer problems if everyone would pray before voting in a business meeting.

Bullies

Some people try to influence others by being a bully. Bullying is a problem in some of our churches today. We have personally experienced it and so have some of our pastor friends. Bullies come in many forms, just like in grade school. There are obvious ones and then there are ones who are sneaky about it. They can be the sweetest looking people on the outside, but on the inside hides a controlling person who tries to bully others in the church. They sometimes get their way through manipulation of others by intimidating them, especially when dealing with committee members.

Deacon Bob scares the children in his church. He walks around with his chest puffed out, staring at the kids, daring them to make a wrong move. (or what he considers a wrong move). The sad thing is that Bob is over the children's ministry and some of the teachers walk around stiff as boards because of the yelling that he does when children don't act exactly as he thinks they should. People in the church who have noticed this behavior tried to talk to the teachers to see if they wanted help with him. In a private conversation, the teachers were outspoken and gave detailed information about Bob. But they were too frightened to face him with it.

It is a shame for children to be afraid at church. Church is supposed to be a haven for children and adults. It should be a place of peace and comfort for everyone who goes there. Bullies do not see themselves that way. Bob saw himself as a strong disciplinarian, but in all actuality he was being a bully. Standing up to a bully is a hard thing to do, whether we are adults or children, but sometimes it is necessary.

My husband experienced bullying from members of a deacon body. He was called to attend a deacon meeting, supposedly to solve some staff problems. Instead, it was a meeting that felt like an inquisition and made him feel like he was on trial. I was invited also and my husband felt like it would be a good idea for me to attend. I went to the meeting and I didn't stay in the room more than ten minutes.

When my husband walked into the room, the deacons were arranged in a semi-circle and there was an empty chair in the middle of the room. The chairman greeted him, led him to sit in the chair and as he sat down, he noticed a tape recorder on a table in front of him. The chairman pushed record and he started asking him questions from a list that was previously made by the deacons. Several deacons sat there with their arms crossed and their expressions were very unfriendly. That would be intimidating for any pastor and that was the intention of some of the deacons who were present that day.

My husband was asked a number of questions and it was very hard for him to think clearly with all of the tension in the room. He answered to the best of his ability under extreme stress. An unfair aspect of this meeting was that the deacons had met to discuss what was to go on at this particular meeting and my husband was the one who was blindsided. They did the same thing to the youth minister, but with much less intimidation. They were trying to resolve a conflict and didn't understand how to do that.

If that were not enough torture, the result of the meeting was that the deacon body sent out a letter to the entire church and community, which included a list of faults, which they found in their pastor and youth minister. A deacon had asked the church secretary for an address list and on that list were church members, visitors, teens, prospects and children. All the letter did was to gossip about the pastor and youth minister and to spread discord. There was no other reason for that letter to have gone out. The result of the letter was that the church split in two. There were some people who received the letter and they were elated, but it cut the church to the core. There were some people who received the letter and they were as heartbroken as we were. That deacon meeting and letter caused us to have many sleepless nights.

The one ray of light in that situation was that there was a lot of pastoral support and he found several new friends in the congregation. People called and came by to express their sorrow and support. But it made them lose respect for the deacons, although there were some very godly deacons in that group, but they were not ones to go against the other deacons. I think if the godly ones had to do it again, they would choose not to send it. The Sunday before the letter was sent, the attendance was higher than it had been in a while. The church was starting to grow and when the letter went out, it became a black eye in the community and people felt that they couldn't worship in a church like that. A community letter is never the answer because it usually doesn't solve anything. It only lets the town know that there are problems in the church. The church is supposed to be a lighthouse in a dark world, not a breeding ground for fights and feuds.

The church was damaged by that letter as there were two groups, one who loved the pastor, but was disenchanted by the deacons, and the other group who didn't care for the pastor and supported the deacons. There was a group of people who wanted to disband the deacons, but my husband told them that was not the answer, although it was very tempting. It would only hurt the deacons who were seeking God and trying to serve Him. This is a case of a couple of bad apples spoiling the entire bushel.

God knows what we need before we do. Several months before, my husband had booked a southern gospel singing group to sing during morning worship that next Sunday. It was His timing because my husband was filled with so much grief and pain, that he was unable to speak to the congregation that morning. The songs that morning were so filled with encouragement and about fighting and winning spiritual battles. We thank God for those great men who sang those songs that day. We consider them our friends.

My husband tried to speak during invitation and had to hand the microphone back to the singing group because he broke down in tears. The gospel group told my husband later that they wondered why most of the congregation was crying. It was as if we were at a funeral. During that invitation, we looked up and there was a line of encouraging people coming by to hug and encourage us. A couple of ladies even stayed up there on the front row with us to show great support. We will never forget those loving people and they are still friends of ours.

That was a hard time in our ministry, but after we cried a while, we picked ourselves back up, dusted ourselves off and went on with the ministry to which we were called. God brought us through that tough situation. We have to hang on and be strong and trust in the Lord to pull us through. Galatians 6:9 says, "And let us not be weary in well doing: for in due season we shall reap, if we faint not."

Threats

Some church members bully the pastor or other minister with threats. Several years ago, we were at a church where we were threatened. There was a teenager who was visiting our church and he was not the type of person that several of the church members approved of, because he was of a different race. People were not very happy that he was even sitting in the church services. Things were fairly calm until he gave his heart to Christ and wanted to be baptized. One by one, several men of the church went to my husband's office and tried to bully him, telling him if he didn't get rid of the teen, that he would regret it. Some of the people gave details of what they would do to him, to me and our child.

Church bullies can be any gender. I have had experiences with female bullies. At that same church, some of the women were threatening me. One particular time that I recall was when I was standing among a group of women and as the conversation dwindled, they walked away to join other conversations. That is when I noticed an older woman standing to my left. She came closer and, with a smile on her face, told me that if my husband did not get rid of the teenager that they didn't like, that they would "take care of us". I was in a room full of women and no one was aware that I was being threatened, because this woman would wait until the other ladies were out of earshot.

The first time that it happened, I remember just standing there in shock. I was thinking, "Did I hear her correctly?" There I was standing in a room full of people, but quietly being threatened. No one else in the room had a clue of what was going on. I could feel my blood leave my body as fear tried to grip me. As if she could read my expression, she said, "You heard me correctly." Later, other women joined in with the threats, one by one. I was so naïve and shocked to realize that this was happening within a church with people who were supposed to be Christian leaders.

We prayed for God's divine protection while making the decision that would please God, and that was to let the teen keep coming to church and worship God in peace. My husband baptized the teenager with undercover police officers in the service and it made the local news, because no one of that "type" was ever baptized in that church or possibly even in that town. God used this situation to spread the gospel through the news program. The baptism was televised and several people were interviewed and the teen was interviewed and when given the chance to speak, spoke only about his new relationship with Jesus. I don't know if he ever realized the threats that we received. We never spoke to him about it.

Things got hotter after that day and we had to lock the church down as soon as we knew that everyone was safely inside at each service. People would come back with reports of having been threatened in the grocery stores by the same people who had threatened us. Some of those people left the church in fear of what would happen to them if they continued to attend the church and to support my husband.

I had just started working at a local place of business, but I had to quit because of the threats. I couldn't go anywhere alone and I had to call my husband when I would walk to the church, so that he would know that I was on my way and that my daughter and I had made it safely inside. We only lived about 50 yards from the church and walking to the church for every service was stressful for me because my daughter was still a toddler.

I was walking in the parking lot of the church one day and my dog was barking. The man said, "I can take care of that dog for you". I told him that the dog was a member of the family and that would not be necessary. A couple of days later, we found the dog dead outside. That is when we decided that it was time to leave that particular church. Living in a parsonage that was owned by the church was our saving grace. They would not do anything to damage their own house. We were grateful for that.

We quit the ministry for about a year and a half after that. We were exhausted with the threats and wondered if it was worth it. We threw our hands up in frustration and went back into the professional job world. We are grateful to have gotten out of that town alive, but eventually God brought us back into full time ministry. Every time that my husband tried to walk away from his calling, God would pull him back in. My husband has the burning desire to preach God's Word and that doesn't change just because we were having a rough time. Even through personal struggles, God always brought us back to be used for His purpose. Sometimes we have failed and made incorrect decisions, but we have learned from those mistakes.

I am sharing these stories to give you a picture of some of the things pastors and their wives go through in the ministry. We try our best to obey God, but we have learned through the years that there are church members that do not play by the rules. When I get upset about the unfair treatment, I usually say, "the rules are different", because some church members feel that we have to use a different set of rules than they do, as I have previously mentioned in this book.

Anonymous Letters

Sometimes bullies are cowards and they write anonymous letters, instead of speaking directly to their pastor. One day as my husband arrived at the church, exhausted from lack of sleep over the problems in the church, he noticed that there was a letter in the box outside of the church. The letter had his name on it.

He walked into his office and sat down to read the letter with a feeling of dread in his chest. As he read it, his heart got heavy with disappointment and grief over this person who was not being led by the Spirit of God. The letter proved that point very clearly as one of the first lines of the letter was "get your -___ out of town before you are run out of town." The letter mentioned other people in it also, but it was filled with venom and not one ounce of love. The fleshly part of my husband wanted to read it from the pulpit, but he refrained because he knew that it would not accomplish anything. It would also give the person attention for what they had done. To this day, they probably wonder if my husband ever received the letter. We just prayed for them and waited for God to take care of it. The letter didn't run us out of town, it only made us pray harder.

It is not a good idea to try and bully a pastor with anonymous letters. They hold no clout with a pastor because the person is not brave enough to come forward and speak to him face to face. It is a coward's way of communicating. They will not get anywhere with him by doing that. They usually do not run off a pastor and the letters sometimes have the opposite response. A pastor who receives that type of letter would probably just dig his heels in, pray harder and keep on keeping on.

I wonder if church bullies ever consider pastor's children, especially if they are trying to run off their daddy based on hearsay or other people's opinions. People would rather join a bully than to be the target of one. Most people who are trying to run off a pastor have not taken the time to get to know him or his family.

My friend and her pastor husband are facing a situation in their church where a very small group of people are trying to gather enough people to get him fired. His wife is devastated by this as this affects his livelihood and it is even harder because they live in a parsonage. If they succeed, not only will the pastor not have a salary anymore, but they will have no place to live. I pray for them that God will prevail and show Himself strong to them in their time of need. God will definitely bring them through this and then eventually either change the people or deliver the pastor from the situation.

Fear

Remember the saying, "If you can't beat them, join them?" This is not good advice when it comes to gossipers or troublemakers. The fear of becoming a target can cause a person to fall under the influence of naysayers. I Corinthians 15:33 says, "...Evil communications corrupt good manners." Manners means ethics or morals and communications means companionship, so in other words, evil companionships corrupt good ethics or morals. Oftentimes, well-meaning people are dragged down, instead of the negative people changing their ways.

We might think that if we join the evil speakers then maybe we will not be the target of their tongues. Maybe they will leave us alone if they think we are one of them. Chances are if they are speaking to you about others, then they are speaking to others about you. Don't join them. It is not worth it and you will also get the same reputation that they have.

If you have heard about their reputation, then you can be sure that others have also. You will be judged by the company you keep. Even if you are not participating in the aggressive speech, you are still guilty by association in the eyes of other people.

Some people have trouble standing up to other people, because it will bring attention to them. Maybe the offending person would get loud and make a scene, and some of us just simply lack the courage. It takes a strong person with strong convictions to stand up to gossips. Again, be an example and just quietly walk away or change the subject. You might lose their friendship, but maybe you will be drawn to some other person who is a true and godly friend.

Powerful People

A lady walked up to a new pastor's wife during their first week there, and took her hand and put $200.00 in her hand. She said it was just a blessing, that's all. Later they found out that she and her husband were in the habit of buying the loyalty of others.

Some people use their wealth to get people, even pastors, to get them to do what they want in the church. Some people are influenced by people who are very powerful in one way or another. Some power is assumed because they are wealthy or influential in the community or in the church. You might think that if you agree with that person, that their success will spill over into your life. Jesus was never influenced by people with earthly wealth and power. Jesus sought out the sick, poor, hurting and broken hearted. He chose to spend time with and minister to people that no one else had any use for. Jesus was living on the earth, but was in a heavenly mindset. We need to follow His example in doing that. I am speaking to myself here too, because I tend to look at my earthly circumstances, instead of my heavenly destination.

Negativity and Complaining

People who speak habitually negatively can be influential to others. Negative speaking is very dangerous and sets up a very volatile and upsetting atmosphere. I know people who do not like their pastor and when asked why, they say that they just don't like him. I found out later that it was because their small group of friends didn't like him or he wasn't like the last pastor, and so they just joined in. After hearing the constant negative influence, they started seeing things in him that they wouldn't have otherwise noticed. Also they were looking at their pastor with eyes tainted with the negativity of their friends. I know a couple of families that no matter who they are talking to they bring up negative things about others, in a very repetitive manner.

Griping and complaining is an enormous problem in our churches. Philippians 2:14-16 says, "Do all things without murmurings and disputing, that ye may be blameless and harmless, the sons of God, without rebuke, in the midst of a crooked and perverse nation, among whom ye shine as lights in the world; Holding forth the word of life; that I may rejoice in the day of Christ, that I have not run in vain, neither laboured in vain."

1 Corinthians 10:10 says, "Neither murmur ye, as some of them also murmured, and were destroyed of the destroyer." The Greek word for murmur means "to murmur, mutter, grumble, say anything against in a low tone."

There was a hair dresser who was so consistently negative that she wound up losing her job. Customers who went into the shop had no choice but to hear her negative opinions about people. Her attitude of telling anyone who would listen made them wonder if she was speaking about them after they left the shop. Her bad reputation cost the salon customers and even though she was asked to leave and move on, she has not realized it and still continues the same behavior, just in another location.

Some people are truly not happy unless they are complaining about something or someone. Be aware of your surroundings and do not fall into the trap of listening to or becoming negative due to the influence of others. If we are around that type of behavior enough, then we might begin to think that it is normal.

Think on positive things and positive things will come out of your mouth. Philippians 4:8 says, "Finally, brethren, whatsoever things are true, whatsoever things are honest, whatsoever things are just, whatsoever things are pure, whatsoever things are lovely, whatsoever things are of good report; if there be any virtue, and if there be any praise, think on these things".

The words "good report" jump out at me when I read this. This means to think on things that people say or "report" to us that are positive, especially things that God has done in their lives. If someone speaks negatively to us, then we have the choice as a listener (the responsibility of the listener) to walk away or to speak up. But do not think on the negative things. Do not dwell on those things because they will only depress and discourage you. Also those thoughts will take your focus off of the things of Christ and put them on negative things.

Flattery

We need to be careful not to be influenced by flattery. There is a difference between a sincere compliment and flattery. A sincere person gives true compliments, but a flatterer is not so sincere.

The Bible says in Psalms 12:3, "The Lord shall cut off all flattering lips, and the tongue that speaketh proud things." Psalms 5:9, "For there is no faithfulness in their mouth; their inward part is very wicked; their throat is an open sepulcher; they flatter with their tongue."

Psalms 12:2 says, "They speak vanity every one with his neighbor, with flattering lips and with a double heart do they speak." This is a picture of a wicked person and it is an example of our tongues speaking what is in our hearts, our very inward parts. Flattery is not sincere praise, but compliments given to influence or manipulate another person into liking you or to get them to see your point of view. This scripture also says that there is no faithfulness in their mouth.

Someone who flatters to get you on their side could drop you in a heartbeat if the tide changes or they decide to go in a different direction. They will find people to flatter and get them on their side, for they are not loyal people. This scripture is a warning to us to stay away from that type of person, or better yet, run as fast as you can in the other direction. You will not find a true and faithful friend in a flatterer. There is a difference in giving true compliments to another person, but flattery is insincere. Don't be influenced by a flatterer and don't get caught up in the habit of being one either.

Committee Influence

Some people try to influence each other in order to get their way. As pastor's wives, sometimes God puts us where He wants us in order to help our husbands to not be blind-sided by people in the church. On a Wednesday night after church, I went to the parking lot to help a lady carry some items to her car. As I was walking, I saw movement so I looked over to my left. In the dark, almost at the back of the building were several men standing there outside of their vehicles. It just happened to be members of the committee that I knew that my husband was going to meet with a few minutes later. That is what several people there called a "parking lot" meeting. Those types of meetings were referred to quite often at that particular church.

I went into the building and I saw my husband coming down the hall going the opposite direction heading outside. I said, "Parking lot meeting beside the building at the back." He knew what I meant and headed straight back to where they were and talked to them for a few minutes, basically letting them know that he saw them and knew what they were up to.

The word spread that I warned Mike about the secret meeting prior to the real meeting. They didn't advertise the sneaky meeting but they had no problem spreading that I had warned him. The word should have spread that they were having a secret parking lot meeting, making decisions about what was going to be discussed in the meeting. By the time committee members got to the meetings, all of the decisions were made. I do not regret warning my husband, because I am here to support him and to warn him of things that I see. I have prayed for God to put me where and when He wants me to be in order to discern deception. If I find out something I feel he needs to know, I will share it with him.

A word to pastors' wives: We are not immune to being influenced or influencing others in a negative way. Be careful with whom who you surround yourself. If you see that they influence in a negative way, don't befriend them and do not trust them. Try to be an example to them and to minister to them when you get a chance. In my experience, true and loyal friends are few and far between. You might have plenty of sweet ladies who are acquaintances and who you can have fun with, but do not freely share your innermost secrets to just anyone, no matter how nice they seem.

Whenever I meet someone new, I listen to the "red flags", which is simply an uneasiness which comes over me about that person. Those flags are generally accurate and we need to be sensitive to them. That doesn't mean that we should ignore that person, but we need to keep a relationship with them at an impersonal level.

There are some people that will not like you no matter what you do, especially if they are being influenced by someone else. Don't exhaust your efforts trying to get people like that to like you. Be kind to them, but don't waste your best hours jumping through hoops. Their minds are set, unless the Holy Spirit changes their minds. I have tried to go out of my way to make some people like me, until I learned to just be myself and know that God loves me and that my worth is in Him. My self-worth used to be in what people thought about me or the way that they treated me. They have to be willing to change because God has given them free will.

Healthy Influence

Pastors' wives: We need to surround ourselves with positive people who do not bring us down and we need to strive to be a good example and a good influence on other people, even the trouble makers. Pray for others and reach out to them whenever you can. Make sure that the Holy Spirit is the major influence in your life and not what pleases everyone else. Please God no matter what.

My life has been influenced in a positive manner by Karol Ladd, who is the author of several books, one of which is called, *The Power of A Positive Woman*. This particular book made a huge impression on me. Her book made me realize how my negativity was a way of life for me. After meeting her and reading her posts on her website, I now find things to speak positively to people at church, especially the elderly people who need to hear our sweet comments.

I encourage you to check out Karol Ladd's website at *www.PositiveLifePrinciples.com*, and get a copy of some of her books and share them with your friends. Let's strive to be a positive influence on others.

My mother is also a positive influence on me and my children. She thinks positively even when the situation looks grim. She lost her husband at a young age and also a dear friend of hers a few years later. She just kept waking up every morning and putting one foot in front of the other and she refused to give up. She strives to please God and to help others as often as she can. That has been an inspiration to me and I am grateful for her positive influence in my life.

Questions To Ponder

1. Have I let unhealthy influences affect my behavior toward others?
2. Have I let influences come between myself and my relationship with God?
3. Have I influenced others to be negative toward someone else?

Father, please forgive me for negatively influencing others or letting others influence me. Please help me to be a positive influence on others and to be an example of your love to them.

CHAPTER 6

Inside The Parsonage

Bill finally made it home. He walked up through the garage to the side door and cautiously opened it not sure what state his wife would be in. It was eerily quiet as he walked through the house wondering where she could be. He could smell something cooking so he knew she was around. He thought to himself, "Maybe she's in the back yard or even next door at the church."

Judy screamed and dropped the basket of clothes she was carrying. Just as he had rounded the corner of the hall he nearly ran into her. She was listening to music on her headphones and didn't hear him come in.

"I'm sorry! I didn't mean to scare you," He said with a chuckle.

She slapped him on the shoulder as he bent over to pick up the basket for her. Her arms were folded and she maintained a serious look. Bill realized that with everything going on she was very sensitive and vulnerable. He kissed her on the cheek and said again he was sorry. She relaxed a bit and said it was alright.

They discussed their day and both felt encouraged by the support they were receiving. Judy told Bill that two other ladies had called during the day just to say they loved them and were praying for them.

A few days later, Judy was at home preparing to go and pick up the kids from school and she jumped at the sound of the phone ringing. Lately, the sound of the phone ringing caused a dread to overcome her. For a split second she hesitated to answer it, wondering if it will be a demand or a complaint.

She checked the caller I.D. and saw that it was the school calling. Her daughter's teacher called to ask her to come by their daughter, Abby's classroom when she came to pick up the kids from school.

Judy arrived and parked near the intermediate building where her daughter's classroom was. As she walked into the room, Judy saw each her children hanging around in the classroom and noticed that her oldest daughter had been crying. Her eyes were red and she was holding a box of tissues that the teacher had given to her.

Her little boy, Timothy, who was in the first grade, ran up and hugged Judy. "Mommy! Abby's crying," he proclaimed.

Judy felt a surge of fear and bewilderment. After she comforted Abby for a few moments, her teacher asked Judy to step into the teacher's lounge with her for a few minutes. She followed her out of the classroom and they sat down on the couch in the lounge.

"Judy, Abby is upset because one of her little church friends came up to her in the hallway between classes and told her that she was sorry to hear about her daddy. Abby stopped in the hallway and asked her what she meant by that and her friend said that she was sorry that the church was firing her daddy," the teacher explained. Abby had gone straight to her teacher because she had taken Abby under her wing and treated her like she was one of her own children.

Judy sat back on the couch, stunned at what she was hearing as tears began to fill her eyes. "I can't believe that a child would be privy to such gossip. She had to have heard it from an adult. Poor Abby. I'm sick that she had to hear that." Judy explained as little as she could to the teacher, explaining that it is just gossip and probably just a rumor. Judy thanked her and walked back to the classroom to take her daughter home from school. The teacher hugged them both and said that she would be praying for them.

Judy thought to herself as she walked to the car, "I can't believe that grown adults would say things like that in front of their children. Don't they realize the damage they can cause to a child about God and church? Some people are simply training their children how to criticize and ruin a church. No wonder churches are more divisive these days than years ago. They're passing the traits down to the next generation."

When Judy got home she went into the bathroom and cried for a while, trying to imagine the pain her daughter must have experienced. When she came out of the bathroom the doorbell rang.

"What now, she thought to herself.

When she opened the door she was relieved to see Marge standing there with a wide smile and a home baked pie in hand. Marge spent the afternoon helping Judy cook dinner for the family as she shared her heart. Marge was always a comfort and reminded Judy of her grandmother growing up. By the time Bill came home Judy was in a more pleasant mood, though still had frustrations.

As good as the support seemed to be, Bill was still disturbed within. He couldn't help but still feel hurt and betrayed, but rather than the desire to be confrontational, he felt a calm assurance encouraging him that regardless of what happens God would take care of him and his family.

For the next few nights Bill slept restlessly. He woke up often with his mind racing with all sorts of doubts and concerns. He knew he should simply trust God and block his mind, but he found it was easier to preach that than it was to practice it.

During the sleepless nights he would find himself drawn to various passages in Psalms. Somehow the words of David gave him comfort, knowing that David experienced greater persecution and threats. Occasionally Judy would join him and they would stay up till morning talking, praying and crying together.

The lack of sleep and concentration as well as a poor appetite began to take a toll on Bill. He was out making visits and his mind seemed to be mesmerized as he ran through a stop sign unaware. The sound of a horn and screeching tires snapped him out of his trance. Fortunately no accident occurred but Bill was shaken and pulled over. He placed his head on the steering wheel and began weeping and crying out to God.

"God, I can't serve you like this! I can't sleep. I don't know who to trust. I'm concerned about my family and the church is hurting. I can't live like this. Please help me!" He cried.

It was at that moment that Bill felt the presence of God and heard the Spirit speak to him.

"My son, Rest in Me. I will take care of you and your family. The church belongs to me and I can take care of them too. You preach my word and feed my sheep. Love those who will let you and trust Me for the outcome."

Bill reached for a box of tissue that he kept in his car. He wiped his eyes and headed to the church. There was a renewed peace and confidence that he had not experienced since this torturous event began. He had finally had a breakthrough. Whatever the outcome, God was able to take care of His own.

There is such a strong excitement when a pastor search committee is looking for a pastor. During the process, the pastor and the committee are trying to make a decision to see if the relationship is a great fit. Remember that your new pastor, his wife and children are moving to a new and strange town or community. They do not know anyone except the committee and maybe a few other people. The children will have a new place to live, a new bedroom, new church children and a new school and classmates to get to know. This can be completely overwhelming to a child, as they wonder if they will be liked and accepted at the new place. They are also leaving friends behind at the prior church and they will be apprehensive and nervous and a bit sad. Give them the time to get to know their new surroundings before expecting too much of them.

Give your new pastor's wife a fair chance. The unknown is scary to her and her family. You are new to her. She will need time to unpack her boxes and get organized, so give her the space that she needs to acclimate herself and her family. Be patient with her as she learns her way around the church, the town and also the names and personalities of church members. You only have to remember the names of the pastor's family, but she will have dozens of names to learn. You only have one family to welcome into the new church. For the first few weeks, she may not be ready to attend every meeting and party that is scheduled at the church. She needs time to get her bearings. She will probably be quiet and just observe for a little while until she finds her place in her new atmosphere.

Her husband will probably hit the ground running and won't

be able to help unpack, so it would be a nice welcome for you to go and offer to help her to unpack and get organized. When we first came to our present church, a sweet church lady came and brought us maps to the town and that was so helpful. Other ladies came later to help me unpack more of the boxes and to organize the house. The pastor search committee went to the local chamber of commerce and supplied us with a kit which included the information that we would need to find just about anything that we would need. It had information about the town, the utilities, the schools, and the local town events and town celebrations.

Your pastor's wife will not be like the last one that you had. She will probably not look like her, act like her or attend the same functions. They will have different priorities and different household situations. She might not work with the same groups as the last one, like children or youth, etc. Get to know her as a person and do not compare her to prior pastor's wives or other staff wives. She will not organize and keep the house exactly as the prior ministers. She will probably not have the same friends as the last pastor's wife. I have noticed that the people I tend to get close to were not friends with the last pastor's wife. It could be because of personalities or that her friends might still be sad about her leaving.

I was told by a lady at one church that she couldn't get to know me because she was so close to the last pastor's wife and she didn't want to get hurt again. She didn't want to be hurt, but it hurt me to hear that because I was drawn to her and would have liked to have gotten to know her. Getting to know her was one of the things that I was looking forward to as we arrived at the church. A couple of years later, she came to me and apologized for that, but the months had already passed without having a relationship with her and I had a generally uncomfortable feeling around her.

Your new pastor's wife might be grieving over having to leave her friends at the last church. It was so hard for us to leave the precious people who became part of our family. At every new church we went to, I went to the church thinking that I couldn't possibly love anyone as much as I loved the ones that I was leaving. But, after a few weeks, the people creep into our hearts and lives and we fall in love with our sweet new church family. It is a great feeling to know that we have life-long friends at every church to which we have been. I have heard that we take a part of everyone we love at each church with us as we move forward into the future.

Sometimes your new first lady will not always be able to attend every meeting and function of the church, especially if she has children. She is generally expected to be at every women's' meetings, church services, parties, wedding and baby showers, funerals and birthday parties. It is easy for her to become overwhelmed and burned out. She doesn't have the luxury of just staying home from church because she is simply exhausted. Her husband is the pastor, not her, so we need to understand that she will do what she can and be where she feels she needs to be at that time.

One Sunday morning, Carrie got her children and husband ready for Sunday school and held back the tears as she watched them walk across the parking lot and into the church building. After they disappeared from her sight, she breathed a deep sigh of relief to finally be alone and she went and sat down on the couch in the parsonage. She held her head in her hands as she released the tears she had been holding in so that her children would not see them. Feelings of isolation and loneliness filled her entire body as she sobbed uncontrollably.

Carrie had been overwhelmed for months with the pressures of being a pastor's wife. She had tried to open up to other women in the church, but they were so busy and only interested in asking for her advice. She asked herself, "Can I bear this lonely life much longer? Why doesn't anyone care or hear me when I cry out for help? Can't they see that I am a real person with real feelings?" She took out a pen and paper and slowly wrote a note to her family, almost with robotic motions, apologizing for what she was about to do. She had reached the end of her rope and felt that she couldn't go on for another minute.

Sadly, she committed suicide in the parsonage of the church, a place where people come to them for help and refuge. She had felt hopeless and exhausted. She appeared to have everything that she could ever want: a loving husband, great kids and a nice home. Her feelings of rejection made her heart ache with longing for a close friendship.

Why doesn't anyone understand the pressures of being a pastor's wife? Maybe her husband received a threatening letter or she had been ridiculed for the last time. Her family lived hours away from her, and her husband had been so busy with the constant demands of the church people. This story might seem unbelievable to you, but this sort of thing does happen, even to pastor's wives.

Remember, your pastor's wife is human! Give her the freedom to be herself and to make mistakes, just as everyone else. She will learn from her mistakes, just as you do. Let her know that she is not alone and she has a church family that she can go to for love and support.

Your first lady will have some very dark times in her life and she needs love and support to get through those times. You will usually see her on Sundays walking around in the church smiling and asking people how they are doing, while her heart is broken.

I have experienced dread on Saturday nights, knowing that I would have to be at church on Sunday morning. Several pastors' wives I know feel the same way as the weekend approaches and they get closer to Sunday. There are so many Sunday morning pressures on a pastor's wife.

Allow her to have natural emotions just like every other lady in the church. There have been many times when I was sitting on the couch in the church parsonage, with my head in my hands, sobbing and crying out to God for solace. My husband didn't even know about these times. Sometimes it was due to cruel words from someone, feelings of loneliness, or even from stressful situations in the church.

Picture your pastor's wife sitting in her home (or in some cases, the church's home) crying her eyes out. She may never share with you that she does. Ask yourself if there is something that you can do to make her life easier and maybe even enjoyable. I will attempt to share some of the things that you can do. You can make a difference in her life and that will help your pastor also. He can do his job a lot easier if he knows that people are caring for and checking on his wife.

We have to share our pastor husbands with many people every day, and we do not see them very much due to the various needs of church members. Remember that pastor's wives have needs too and one of them is for her to spend time with her husband.

One thing that you can do for her is to try to give him time with her and their children. Try not to call him in the evenings and on holidays unless it is absolutely necessary. Give them time to eat supper together as a family or maybe play basketball or something outside. My husband feels guilty whenever he is outside playing with the kids, especially if a church member drives by and sees him. He feels that he should be doing something with the church, but he realizes that his children want to spend time with him. He realizes that people have needs and he wants to be there to meet them, but in order for him to be effective at his job, he needs some down time.

If you call your pastor and ask him to go and visit your friend or relative, realize that you are not the only one who is possibly calling him. Sometimes it might take him a while to get to the hospital, depending on what he is doing at the time that you called. He visits church members, but sometimes he is asked to visit people who are not members of the church and some people he has never met. Sometimes they even have a pastor from another church visiting them. Try to be sensitive to his schedule and if a deacon can go and visit them, you might call a deacon to go and visit until the pastor can get there.

I want to proclaim something to all church members everywhere. Are you ready? Here it comes! Pastors and their wives cannot read your mind. They cannot see into your homes and know your schedule of events to know when you are having surgery or when you might need a home visit. If you or someone else doesn't tell him, chances are he will not be there for you.

My husband and I were on our way home from a hospital visit in a town that was about an hour away from our home. As we were leaving the city to return home, my husband received a phone call saying that a man from the church had surgery that morning and that he was on his way home from the hospital. It was, in fact, the very hospital we had just left. My husband called the man's house a little later and apologized to him for not being at the surgery and told him that he didn't know about it. The man told my husband that he had mentioned it to a deacon in the church and that deacon said that he would tell my husband about the surgery. The deacon even saw and spoke to my husband the night before the surgery and never mentioned it. The man thought that the pastor had received the message and just didn't go to see him. If you want him to be there, then ask him and if he is free, he will probably accommodate you.

Sometimes a pastor might have to choose between a surgery that is life-threatening and a surgery that is not as serious. He absolutely cannot be in two places at once. He is just like any other person.

Your pastor probably makes the job look easier than it actually is. Be patient and wait for him to get a spare moment to go and visit you or your family and friends. He might actually have someone sick at his home. There should be a balance between church duties and family responsibilities. He does not have super powers and needs his rest and relaxation.

A pastor's schedule is so unpredictable, so it is a challenge for him to make time for his family and to study when so many other people need him or think they need him. My husband teaches a Sunday school class and preaches every Sunday morning and also on Sunday nights and then he teaches on Wednesday nights. He spends approximately 8 or 9 hours of study time for each sermon that he preaches, so that is a weekly minimum of 24 to 27 hours per week. That is not including prayer and meditation time.

Pastors go to every church service, funerals, weddings, hospitals, nursing homes and home visits. Most people in our area use a hospital that is over an hour away. I am listing these things to let you know the enormous responsibility and expectations that are on a pastor every week. He has to leave town in order to get any time off, because even when he is off, he is on call, even on holidays and vacations. Please take this into consideration the next time you have the urge to pick up the phone and ask him to visit someone or to spend time with your family.

The pastor cannot possibly visit every single member of the church, so he has to decide who needs him the most. Some people get angry if the pastor doesn't go and see them every week. One home bound lady wouldn't even receive the sermon cd because he had not gone to see her in three weeks. Other people needed him during those three weeks. She just wanted to chat.

We understand that people are lonely and we try to help whenever we can, but that is where church members can take the pressure off of the pastor. They can go and visit some of these sweet and lonely church members and keep them happy while the pastor is out doing his other duties. If someone is very strongly on your mind, then that might be God urging you to go and tend to that person instead of picking up the phone and calling your pastor. If we all work together, then that will make life easier on your pastor and meet everyone's needs.

Missing her extended family is a reason that your first lady might be crying in the parsonage. Pastor's wives follow their husbands wherever God leads them. This is very tough on a woman emotionally, but she wants to serve God and to support her husband, and she gets homesick for her friends and family. She probably misses the familiarity of her hometown. It is hard to be away from family, especially if there is an emergency back home.

Oftentimes, due to her husband's duties, she and the kids will have to travel to be with her family. She cannot just pop over to her mom's house for Sunday dinner. I have not been to a family reunion in many years because they are held on Sunday afternoons and I miss the annual family Christmas party every year also. That is the sacrifice we make and we realize the importance of being where God has planted us for each season in our lives.

You might want to invite the pastor and his family to your house for a meal, especially on holidays. Mother's Day and Easter are important days for a pastor to be at the church and that sometimes means that they will not have any family around during those times.

Care for Her

When we first went to a prior church, we were invited over for dinner at the Chairman of Deacon's home. After we finished eating and were just sitting around the table chatting, the deacon's wife said that they just wanted to love us, if we would let them. That statement brought tears to my eyes. After being hurt at our prior church, it was scary to risk letting people get too close. As she said that, I saw genuine love and concern for us as people, not just as their new pastor and his wife. I felt an affection for that couple that very day, since then, we have felt nothing but love from both of them and their son, who is also a deacon in the church. I was able to share with her how much that one statement meant to us.

At our last church and the one before that, there were several ladies who still remain special to me as they showed me that they loved me. They listened to me, prayed with me and brought us cakes and food to show us that they cared for us. I still keep in contact with them and I love them dearly. They will be friends for life.

If you hear that your preacher's wife is sick or if she has had surgery, it would warm her heart if you would bring her soup, jello, or call and ask her if she needs any help with her children. She might be too sick to do her dishes or sweep her floor. She needs to be taken care of while her pastor husband is out taking care of the church folks. I cannot express the tremendous relief when I am sick and a sweet person in the church shows up with soup. It makes me feel loved and appreciated.

We were at a church a few years ago where people there would bring us wonderful meals. Sometimes it was because they had heard that one of us was sick, but other times, it was just to be nice. It warmed our hearts, not to mention our stomachs. We felt so loved and wanted and since my children were small, it took a lot of pressure off of me to be able to feed them, especially while I was sick. We were spoiled at that church. I had a friend that I would walk with and we would talk and there were other people who would just sit there with me when I was upset. I could call a number of people any time of the day or night and they would not hesitate to be there. That is what constitutes a family and close friends. I had surgery at a hospital that was over an hour away from our church and home and several people went there to visit me and one friend even spent the night. They will always be family to me. Even at our present church, I have already found a few ladies whom I enjoy spending time with.

Years ago, when I had surgery, several people pitched in to help us. Some came over and swept and mopped and others helped with my small children. I was able to relax and try to recover because of their selfless acts to us. I miss them so much and we still try to see each other every time we can.

Calling to tell your pastor's wife that you love her and that you are praying for her would mean the world to her. But most importantly, pray for her on a daily basis as she helps and supports her husband. You might just let her know that she is on your mind or send her a card of encouragement. Sometimes we wonder if we are really making a difference in the church and our town.

Pastor's wives are often a target of careless words said about her or her children, not to mention her husband. She might not ever tell you about it, but she will cry out to God in the church parsonage. If you hear people being negative about her, take a stand and remind them that she is human and that she hurts like everyone else.

We are also affected by what is said and done to our husbands. It is hard for a wife to watch her husband struggle with the effects of damaging words to him or his family. We watch them being abused or ridiculed and we feel so helpless when they have many sleepless nights due to offenses or complaints. Wouldn't you hate to be the very one who keeps your pastor awake at night? Don't be the person that causes your pastor or his wife to lose sleep or to dread going to church or to meetings. Don't be that one who makes him want to run the other direction when he sees you.

There are many reasons for a pastor and his wife to lose sleep, unresolved conflict and threats being two major ones. Concentrate on being the person that encourages and lets them know that you pray for them. Be the one who, after they move away, they will miss and cannot wait to go back and visit. Be a blessing in every way that you can and encourage peace within the members. Be the one who encourages him and his wife and lets them know that they are not alone in the ministry.

Everywhere we go, we find people who are special to us and we keep them close in our hearts even when we are separated by many miles.

It is so easy to judge someone if you have never walked in their shoes. Your pastor's wife is not sitting at home eating chocolate and watching movies all day. She might choose to stay at home with her children and not work outside of the home, but don't assume that she is not busy.

Being a mom is very hectic and rewarding, even to pastors' wives. If you could see inside of her house, you would see the activity that is normal in almost every household, including homework, cooking meals, washing clothes, taking care of the children, etc.

The Phone

Answering the phone in a pastor's home is often a job in itself. People call the pastor's home at all hours of the day and night, and we realize that we are there for emergencies or questions. It can be stressful for a pastor or his wife to miss a call.

There are church members who think that the parsonage phone should be answered at all times. But, there are times we are away from the phone, maybe taking a shower, going to the store, or going outside with the children.

The pastor and his wife are not just sitting there staring at the phone waiting for it to ring so that he can spring into action.

Be in the habit of leaving a message telling what you need and they will surely get back in touch with you whenever they are able. Due to the number of calls that we receive, we limit the return calls to people who actually leave us a message. We try to get to everyone as soon as possible. Sometimes I get to the place where I cringe when the phone rings because my husband is so swamped already. I wonder where he will get the time to do whatever that person needs.

Your pastor's wife might be in the parsonage sending out cards, typing letters, preparing for ministry events, encouraging someone on the phone or in person. She could be cooking and cleaning for her family. Pastor's wives wear several hats as wife, mother, secretary, accountant, counselor and fielder of complaints and problems. A pet peeve of mine is to hear someone say, "Let the pastor's wife do it. She doesn't do anything all day." Follow her around for a week or two and you will see what she does behind the scenes. She probably won't get up in front of the church and boast about everything that she has done that week.

Don't Take It Out on Her

It is not fair to unload our anger on the pastor's wife about her husband. If we are offended by him, then we need to go directly to him. Chances are very good that his wife wouldn't know what we are speaking of anyway and she cannot answer for him until she has had the time to talk to him about it. The disgruntled person has usually planned and prepared the list of complaints about her husband and they have had time to get ready for it. The pastor's wife was not prepared for the conversation because she didn't know that it was going to take place. This is so unfair.

I cannot count the times that I have been told to tell my husband one thing or another. People have given me messages to give my husband, usually starting the sentence with, "You go and tell that husband of yours..." People need to go to their pastor and share it with him and spare her the grief. When someone takes out their anger and frustrations out on his wife, it not only hurts him, but it hurts her too. She will then have to make a decision of whether to share those things with her husband. There have actually been times where I have not shared those things with my husband. I try to tell the person to go and talk to him directly.

We received a letter one time and I read it and just threw it away to spare him the pain that person was trying to inflict. Sometimes he just doesn't need to know if it is only going to cause him distraction from what he needs to be doing.

I have been cursed at in the middle of a church service because a lady did not like the greeting time, where people shake hands with each other. I went over to her to shake her hand and she told me what she thought of it, while cursing at me. She should have gone to my husband, but instead of telling him, she told me. I remember opening my mouth and then closing it again, speechless, thinking, "did I just hear what I thought I heard?" As if she could read my mind, she said, "You heard me right. I did say that." I was upset as that was my first time being cursed at by a church member. After the service was over, I told my husband and he called her. Instead of denying it, she repeated the statement, curse words and all, for my husband.

The very next day, she had a heart attack and was rushed to the hospital. Upon hearing the news about her, my husband and I didn't hesitate to drive over an hour away to see her in the intensive care unit. He was just as caring to her as he would have been to anyone else. I am not trying to say that it was easy to do that, but God gives us grace to be able to do the right thing.

Psalms 39:1 says, "I will take heed to my ways that I sin not with my tongue; I will keep my mouth with a bridle while the wicked is before me." This is a picture of someone who is faced with a wicked person, yet will not respond to them in a hostile manner. We should all memorize this scripture and say it to ourselves when faced with a person who is trying to hurt us or to manipulate us.

I have stood in front of people lashing out at me or to me about my husband and I didn't have an appropriate response or sometimes I responded too hastily. I have learned to just listen to them and then to just walk away.

My husband has had to walk away from conversations like that and also had to walk out of a deacon meeting in order to refrain from lashing back at one of the deacons who had chosen to pick a fight. The meeting was over and it seemed to be a calm one but then he started a bashing session against my husband. He told the deacon that he didn't have to stand there and listen to him before walking out. My husband felt guilty but it kept him from saying something he might regret.

The Rules Are Different

The rules are not the same for pastors as for church members, although they should be. After we get a moment to speak with our husbands, we can find out what is going on and then get him to go and talk to you. When I am confronted, I usually do not have a ready response and I need time to digest the information and to pray about it. Sometimes I cannot get a word in with the angry person.

When a church member gets angry, they come to us and release their venom without holding back to spare our feelings. They walk away from the conversation feeling much better after getting that off of their chest. They leave us feeling discouraged and upset and they go on about their day while we are dealing with the emotions from their venting. Again, the rules are different.

A pastor and his wife are expected to give a godly response even when towered over and intimidated. We try, but we expect the same consideration of church folks. Sometimes I say exactly the wrong thing and when I realize it, I try to make it better by continuing to talk to fix it. It usually just gets worse so I have learned to say that I didn't mean that the way it sounded and then I tell the person what I really meant. It is very humbling to tell someone that I just made a mistake right in front of them. But spending a few extra minutes explaining it usually keeps the person from misunderstanding or getting offended. It is settled right then. I sure wish that I had learned this sooner.

One of the worst times to confront your pastor or his wife is right before a church service. He has to be prayed up and make sure that he is following the leading of the Holy Spirit and that cannot be clouded with negativity. My husband has had people stop him on his way to the pulpit to tell him that they needed to meet with him that week, and oftentimes it was a consistently hostile or volatile person. His mind should be on what he is going to preach, not worrying about what that person wants to speak to him about. It can usually wait until after church to request an appointment with him or his wife. She also needs to be in a positive frame of mind before church services. We need to try to respect the pastor's time for prayer and meditation before he has to preach.

At one church, a deacon stopped, reached out his hand and grabbed my husband's arm as he was going up the aisle to sit down for the song service. The congregation was singing and the deacon told my husband that he needed to talk to him and told him the day and the time. He didn't ask him if he could meet them at that time. He told my husband that he wanted to speak to him then. This particular deacon had been a thorn in his side, so he lost his focus on his sermon and struggled to preach that morning. He was very distracted, knowing he would have a battle later in the week. It turned out to be a very rough meeting. It is better to speak to the pastor after church when he is more relaxed and can focus on what you are saying.

Let Her Be Herself

A very important thing that you can do to make a difference in the life of your first lady is to get to know her as a person and give her a fair chance to become a friend to you. She might even feel isolated as she is away from her family and doesn't know who will give her a chance. At our present church, I have a dear sweet neighbor who just lets me be myself. We can chat about things and I can laugh and just be who I am and she doesn't judge me or criticize me in any way. She likes that I am human, just like she is and she is more relaxed with me. Most importantly, she does not talk about me behind my back. That is so very crucial to a pastor's wife.

Your pastor's wife needs days where she gets to just go shopping or be with the "girls" or a friend whom she enjoys being with. Sometimes we need an outlet that lets us be ourselves that has nothing to do with the church, where there is no one watching or expecting anything. Inside the home is where I can feel that I can be myself and let my guard down.

There are days where I like being at home more than being out and I do not like to spend money. I have incredible buyer's remorse and, much to my husband's dismay, I get to the checkout and start putting things back, especially if it was an impulse buy. I enjoy the simple things like walking with a friend or visiting with them, and at the end of the day, I am usually so glad that I went.

Don't be fooled by your pastor's wife's smiling face every Sunday. She will have rough days, just as you do. She will be devastated at times. There are times that she will fall on her face before God and cry and then she will get up and pull up her boot straps and carry on.

Being a child of God is a battle every day, so we need to fight with our swords, which is the Word of God. We need to study God's word in order to fight the enemy that lay us at the feet of God. There have been tough times in my life where I was so desperate for God's presence and guidance in my life that I was on my face crying huge tears before God. Crying has a cleansing effect and it relieves tension that has built up throughout life's situations.

Your pastor's wife wants to be loved and accepted for who she is, just as you do. Be a friend to her and if she happens to confide in you, then it is very important for you to keep her confidences. She might have personal problems that she cannot talk to just anyone about. There is comfort in finding a lady friend who understands and just lets her let her hair down and be a normal woman for a while.

There have been situations where I did not have a clear answer and needed to run it by someone else to see if I am on the right track. Sometimes a friend would call my attention to something that I had missed or that I hadn't even thought of.

Pastors' Children

Pastors and their wives live in glass houses, but their children are affected by every aspect of the ministry. Remember that preacher's kids (Pks) are not adults and they have ears and can be affected by what you say around them. Even if you do not care for their parents, respect the children. My kids have asked me why certain people hate them, because they believe that if someone is mean to their parents, then they hate them also.

A couple of months after we put our children in a new school, someone who worked at the school stood up and shouted at my husband in a business meeting at church. After that, my daughter was very nervous at school and cried a lot. Both of my children were terrified that they would receive the same treatment as my husband. It took months for them to get over that public display. My children were trying to acclimate to a new school with strangers all around them.

Children think more simply than adults. It is more black and white with them and they do not understand the motives behind words. They just hear what is said and take it to heart. Don't just be careful about speaking around pastors' children, but more importantly, watch what you say TO pastor's children. They are not responsible for what their parents say or do and should not be expected to give an opinion concerning adult matters. Pastor's children have a lot of stress on them to be an example to their classmates at school and at church. They often hear other children say, "I thought you were a preacher's kid". Our children have emotions just like other kids their age. They have ears and can hear what is being said to and about their father and mother. Sometimes we think that our kids don't hear the conversations we have, but they soak in much more than we realize.

It is unacceptable to correct or demean a pastor in front of his children or his wife. This also pertains to his wife. It brings humiliation to the pastor or his wife. I have been in situations where someone walked up and said a hurtful statement to me or my husband, and later one of my children have asked, "Mom, why does that person hate us?" Children take things to heart and when it is said to the mom or dad, they might believe that it includes them.

My daughter was walking down the hallway between classes a couple of years ago, and a little girl stopped her and said that she was sorry about her daddy. My daughter asked her what she was talking about and the girl responded, "That there are people trying to run your daddy off." My daughter was traumatized by this statement and she couldn't concentrate on her school work for the rest of the day. She had crying spells at school for a while, due to the stress of that one statement. This little girl had very good intentions toward my daughter, but the words still cut her deeply. She had obviously heard people in the church talking, because this little girl's parents didn't attend church.

I am grateful there was a godly and caring teacher at school, who treated her as if she were her own child. She encouraged her to open up to her anytime that she needed it. She is a stronger child because of the love shown to her by this teacher.

One day my son was on the playground in elementary school. A child came up to him and made a mean comment to him that he had heard from his parents at home. My little boy didn't understand what he was talking about. It upset him very much. Those little comments are proof that adults are irresponsibly talking about their pastor in front of their small children. That same little boy taunted my son whenever he saw him at school.

He would yell in his ear to move out of his way if he wanted to pass by him. I told my son to ignore it and not to say anything back to him. What confused my son is the fact that this little boy was his friend before his parents disliked his daddy. Because of incidents like these, we now choose to home school them. They do not deserve the negative comments that are pointed in their direction about things that they do not understand.

Pastors' children can feel pressure from the feeling of being viewed through a magnifying glass, just like their parents. Children are much smarter and intuitive than we give them credit. Children need to be able to be themselves in the way they act, talk and dress, without having to worry about pleasing people in the church. They also need the freedom to be human and to enjoy their childhoods just like any other child in the church. These kids have needs and desires that other children have, and they will also argue with their siblings and maybe even have a tantrum along the way. Give them the space to make their mistakes and to overcome them. Encourage them whenever you see them.

It might be nice to acknowledge your pastor's children and make them feel welcome in their new town and their new church. When a new pastor comes to your church, he and his wife will be adjusting to their new environment, but so will their children. They will need the time to get accustomed to new people and new places and, in many cases, a new school. Our children do not know who they can trust to be friends with until they can get their bearings and find other children with the same interests and morals.

One of the things that impressed us about one of our pastorates is that while we were in the initial meeting with the pastor search committee, there were a couple of women who had made plans with our children. They took them to get snow cones and to show them the new town where they might possibly be living. They cared enough to show the children that they were important and that they mattered. That was a great first impression for our children.

Most importantly, I don't want my children to grow up to resent church because of what they have witnessed behind the scenes of church life. I have gotten to know some adult pastors' children, and some of them are resentful and stressed when church is mentioned. They were tired of the fussing and fighting that goes on in many churches today. They run away from church and church people.

I have also seen many pastors' kids who grew up to be godly servants of God who show love and respect to others. I want my children to respect church leaders and other members in the church and in the community. I want my children to continue to hunger for the things of God as they do now.

A Word for You, Dear Pastor's Wife

Keep your head up, dear pastor's wife. Keep putting one foot in front of the other and loving the people, even if they are against you. Speak to them even if you know they are working behind the scenes against you or your husband. Drop your sword and cry if you need to, but definitely lay your burdens at the feet of Jesus and let Him guide you and help you through every situation that comes against you.

I know that things get so heavy sometimes, and you might think that you cannot make it through your present situation. You cannot make it alone, but with God's help and guidance, you can and will make it. Just keep praying and trusting God. Psalms 18:2 says, "The LORD is my rock, and my fortress, and my deliverer; my God, my strength, in whom I will trust; my buckler, and the horn of my salvation, and my high tower."

Proverbs 10:24 tells us that Jesus sticks closer than a brother. There is typically a strong bond between brothers and it is hard to imagine someone being even closer than a brother who loves you so much. Jesus has promised this to His children.

Loving and caring about people is worth the risk of being hurt, just be discerning. People are watching you and how you react to different situations. Be someone that they would want to be like. Make them want the qualities that they see in you. God is with you and He will not leave you helpless or hopeless. You are bought with a price and you are worth everything to God. God loves you and truly desires to bless you and work through you to bring glory and honor to his name.

Even though you might be going through a rough time in your ministry right now, God is still in control and He will deliver you one way or another. Sometimes God leaves you there until another church becomes available and until it is the perfect time for you to go. You might be praying, "GOD please deliver us!" Or "GOD, why aren't you delivering us?" At times we have thought both of those things. We stayed another year after praying that at one church, but looking back we know now that God had a plan and the church we went to was not ready for us yet. God's timing was perfect on that because when we went, they were completely ready for us. It was an easy transition because we were patient and waited on God and trusted Him to move us when He was ready.

Your pastor husband might have to be terminated in order to be delivered. As hurtful as that can be, sometimes it is a blessing in disguise. Termination affects the husband, wife and children. The family has to pick up and move to another town, another house, and another school.

Proverbs 18:24 says, "...there is a friend that sticketh closer than a brother." That friend is Jesus. A brother is family and a relationship with a brother is very close. The scripture says that Jesus sticks even closer than that.

Ultimately, God is in control and He takes care of us. He took care of us while going through the difficult times and He is still watching over us and caring for us. He will never leave us nor forsake us. What a wonderful God!

Questions To Ponder

1. Have I been supportive of my pastor and his wife?
2. Have I been praying for my pastor and his family?
3. Have I been an encouragement to my pastor and his wife?

Father, please forgive me for not encouraging and supporting my pastor and his wife and children. Please remind me to encourage them and reveal to me ways to help my pastor and his wife, so that they can lead us toward You.

Chapter 7

Having Done All, Stand!

Bro. Bill walked into Dinah's office and asked her where Bro. Larry was.

"Oh, he should be down the hall or maybe in the Family Life Center," Dinah responded cheerfully.

"Would you notify him that I'd like to have a meeting with both of you at one o'clock?" Bill asked. "And can you contact Bro. Ted and see if he's available to come in as well?"

"Why I sure will, Preacher."

"Thank you Dinah, I really do appreciate all the work you do around here."

"Why you're so welcome," She said with a hearty grin.

Bill turned and headed toward his office smacking his forehead with his hand. "Why did you say that to her?" he thought to himself. "I really do appreciate all the work you do."

"Really?" he cut his thought off. "Where in the world did that come from? Yeah, she's doing a lot of work around here to make me miserable."

Then his conscience chided him and God spoke to his heart, "I put those words in your mouth. Bless them that curse you."

"Thank you, Lord!" Bill conceded.

He sat at his desk for a few moments and began rehearsing in his mind how he would direct the meeting. Since discovering the truth about Dinah, her cheery countenance no longer deceived him. He could see through her now as if he was looking directly into her heart.

He decided to go into his closet, which doubled as a private prayer room. He got on his knees and prayed for wisdom and guidance in this situation. He knew it was time to try and bring peace to the church and it would begin with the meeting with his staff.

After about twenty minutes of praying and listening, he concluded his praying and waited for the phone call at his desk. As he waited he fumbled through some notes for a sermon series he was preparing, even though his mind was not on a message.

The phone rang and he waited nervously for the transfer.

The intercom buzzed and Bill picked up the phone.

"Bro. Bill, Bro. Frank is on line one," Dinah announced.

"Thank you, Dinah"

Bill quickly pressed line one and answered, "Hey Bro. Frank, how are you today?"

"I'm blessed, Preacher! Is everything set up?"

"Yes sir, Frank. I scheduled it at one o'clock and we should have Bro. Ted here too."

"Great! Ted is a fine man and he's got your back. I already spoke with him and he was able to take off work early so when she calls him, he'll pretend that he doesn't know anything."

"How about you? Are you ready, Bro. Bill?" asked Frank.

"I guess I'm as ready as I'll ever be."

"I will see you in a few hours, Bill."

Bill hesitated to hang up. There was a thought that came to his spirit to listen a little longer before hanging up after Frank had already hung up his line. Bill listened quietly for a moment and he could hear faint breathing on the line and then a click. Just then he saw the light on Dinah's phone line go off. Bill's heart sank again.

It was now confirmed in his mind that everything he had been told was true. This gave him courage to realize that he was doing the right thing and that it was time to deliver the flock from the ravenous wolves.

A few minutes before one o'clock Bill heard voices enter the receptionist area near Dinah's office. He heard even more voices join in and began to wonder who all was now here.

At that moment, Dinah buzzed Bill's intercom and announced that Frank and some other men were there.

"Thanks Dinah, tell them I'll be up there in a moment."
Bill's hands began to shake a bit and he could feel his anxiety rising as he got up from his desk and walked toward the front office. Then things got worse. As he rounded the corner he saw who was waiting with Frank and Henry. Two other deacons were there that Bill was not expecting. It was Sam and Glenn, two of the most difficult deacons in the church.

"I wonder why they are here," Bill asked himself.
Before Bill could reach the group of men Frank met him and whispered to him, "They found out about the meeting. Darned if I know how but they want in so I told them it would be fine. What do you think?"

"I think I know how they found out. Let's do this!" Bill stated with confidence. Bill was wondering inside how he suddenly had a surge of boldness come over him. He realized that God was empowering him during a time of trial.

Bill greeted each of them and asked Dinah to please turn on the phone answering system, lock the exit doors and join them in the conference room.

After they were seated, Frank asked Ted to open with prayer. Henry spoke first sharing concerns of some of the parishioners that have continued to come up. He said that he and Frank wanted to help intervene to see if they could try to clear up any misunderstandings and work together for the good of the church. This meeting was simply preliminary to just get things clear.

Before he could get to some of the precise concerns Sam, who had been leering at Bro. Bill, bellowed in, "I can tell you what the problem is around here. It's that preacher right there. I knew we shouldn't have called him here."

Frank chimed in, "Whoa, Sam, what's this all about? You were on the committee who suggested that he was God's man for our church."

"Well I was misled by his lies," Frank retorted.

"Now just a minute Sam," interrupted Henry. "We're not going to go there. That kind of talk is uncalled for and you are talking about a man of God here."

"He isn't a man of God. I know some things about him that will come out soon enough," Glenn stated.

Glenn was a man who was evidently undereducated, yet was a hard worker. He had been injured some time ago and later survived a stroke and brain surgery. He had a habit of blurting out what he thought and often said things that were gruff and implausible. He always seemed to hover around Sam. If you saw Sam then Glenn wasn't too far. The room became thick at the insinuation Glenn was making.

"What things? What are you talking about?" blurted Bro. Bill. He had heard enough. "If you think I'm going to let you smear my character and integrity-"

"You'll find out soon. When we get through with you, don't be surprised if you aren't the pastor here," Glenn crowed.

Bill later learned that Glenn was known for making empty threats and that he was just trying to cause confusion to the matter.

At that Sam stood up and announced, "This meeting is adjourned. Let's go."

Bill stood and said, "This meeting is not over until I say it's over. This is a staff meeting to iron out some discrepancies. You were not asked to be here and you have no authority to come in here and commandeer this meeting."

Sam puffed out his chest. Being a large size man, he was certainly not used to anybody challenging him much less a young preacher who he had no respect for.

"You can have your meeting but these three are with me. Let's go." Sam pointed to Dinah, Bro. Larry and Bro. Ted. He and Glenn walked out of the room followed by Dinah and Larry.

Ted stayed seated as the men looked around at each other, stunned at the turn of events. He broke the ice by saying, "I don't know that fellow."

The men let out a chuckle and began to release the tension that had surged in that short meeting. Ted knew he had just made a decision as to where he stood and that in the end this could turn out difficult for him as well.

They could hear the rustling of keys and whispers going out the office door. Then they heard clearly as Sam said, "If he's with them then he'll be gone right along with that preacher."

They heard the door close and then silence.

Frank looked at Ted and asked, "Are you okay?"

Ted confessed, "Well, I'm a bit shaken but I've seen this side of him before and I've known for a few months they have been planning to assault Bro. Bill at a business meeting soon. Until you spoke to me, Frank, I didn't know that it was just a small group of folks stirring the pot. According to Bro. Larry, the majority of the church was disgruntled about Bro. Bill."

Ted turned to Bro Bill and said, "I'm sorry that I didn't come to you sooner to find out what was really going on. I don't like it and I believe God sent you here, Bro. Bill. If they run you off then, well, I can't see my family and me staying for what they have planned."

"Well, I appreciate your confidence, Bro. Larry, but I don't want you -"

Henry interrupted Bill, "Guys we need to be ready for next Wednesday."

"What is next Wednesday?" asked Larry.

"Business meeting," answered Frank.

"Do you think they will attempt anything?" asked Bill.

Frank responded, "Well Bill, if they do I think we should be ready. You don't worry about a thing. Keep a low profile and pray. We will take care of notifying the right folks."

"Look Frank, I'm not sure that we should be politicking the way that they are. Shouldn't we just trust God with the outcome?" asked Bill.

"We can do that if you prefer. But before you decide, let me explain why I believe we should pursue this. The folks who just left here will spread misinformation and -"

"Lies!" interrupted Henry.

"That's right; lies and anything else that they can do to gain an advantage to have their way. This is not a war against a few folks but against powers and principalities. It is against the enemy of the cross and all we will be doing is holding prayer meetings and informing folks to be prepared if need be to defend the church and their Pastor and his family. We will not share the names of those who are stirring even though they probably already know. Now how does that sound?"

"You make a good case, Frank. I believe it would be wise to begin the praying right now," answered Bill.

The men spent the next twenty or so minutes as each of them

took turns praying. Each one came out of the conference room with red, tear dimmed eyes.

Frank stayed behind a moment to speak with Bill as the others left. He could only imagine the pain and hurt that his pastor was feeling at this moment.

"Bill, I am doing this for several reasons. One of those reasons is because you have become like a son to me. I want you to know that Margaret and I love you and your sweet family a whole bunch."

"Frank, I have come to love you too - a whole bunch."

The two men hugged as Bill began weeping again. As they left, Bill felt the stiff cool breeze of autumn blowing and he began slightly trembling. He thought to himself as he walked home whether it was the cool breeze or his nerves causing the tremors.

Later that evening, Bill spoke with Judy and informed her of the meeting and how things didn't go well at all.

"I guess I should start repacking," Judy sighed.

"Let's hold off for a bit, honey. If things don't work out in our favor, then I'll make sure we have time to relocate."

"Bill, this is no kind of life to raise a family." Judy began getting tearful and sniffling again.

"I know. I am concerned that the kids may despise church altogether, but the ministry is full of challenges, Judy."

"Yeah, but I understood surrendering to the ministry would be challenging if you went to a foreign mission field with savage tribes trying to kill you. These are supposed to be civilized Christians and leaders who are operating in the Holy Spirit," she said in frustration.

"I know, Honey. But remember it was the religious leaders who persecuted Christ and the church. We must dig deep within and count it a joy to suffer for Christ against the darkness of this world, even when it is exposed in the church. God will receive glory if we will trust in Him, no matter the outcome."

"I guess. It's just hard on the kids, and on me and -"

They hugged and Bill whispered a prayer in her ear which helped her feel a little sense of peace.

The next week was basically uneventful. Dinah didn't show up for the rest of the week leading to Sunday, but somehow the bulletins got printed. Larry wasn't in either so it was kind of quiet around the church office.

Bill had thought of calling to check on them, but figured he didn't want to stir things up any further.

Sunday brought the typical crowds with a few more vacancies than usual.

There were some pleasant surprises. Bill and Judy received a few cards of encouragement in the mail and slipped under his door. Two ladies brought a cake and a couple of others brought some casseroles.

Over all with the tension in the atmosphere there was a glimmer of hope and encouragement from several supportive church members.

Wednesday evening came and the mood was very somber. Bill could sense the dark presence creeping into his office just before time for service. As he walked towards the sanctuary, he could see a few folks talking down the hall near the restrooms.

"We have visitors tonight?" he thought to himself. "Not tonight with a business meeting."

As he entered the sanctuary the chatter hit his ears. He looked and the church was packed. A chill went through his spine as he suddenly flashed back to the night that he found the note stabbed into the pulpit.

One by one he began greeting folks as his eyes scanned the auditorium, seeing many faces he didn't recognize.

He found Frank and asked quietly, "What's all this, Brother?"

"Well, Preacher, there appears to be several folks here who haven't been here in ten or twenty years. I don't know how things are going to turn out but this is usually a sign that tonight is the night. I do see a lot of familiar good folks but we'll have to see."

After a couple of songs it came time to call the meeting to order. As Bill called the meeting to order, before he could finish his sentence, he heard some shouting. Caught off guard he asked, "I beg your pardon?"

A short heavy set man stood and shouted, "I move to elect a new moderator."

Bill quickly heard an unseen voice shout, "I second."

Bill looked at the man and asked quite bluntly, "And who are you?"

"I'm James Cook. I grew up in this church. I haven't been here much because I work a lot."

Another voice came up loud and clear and said, "I elect Bro. Frank as the new moderator."

Bill heard "Amen's" and "Second's" ringing forth.

Bill was a little relieved to be able to sit down and watch the proceedings. After all, now Bill will be able to vote on anything that comes up. "If the whole assembly is agreeable, then I will step aside and Bro. Frank can moderate. Do I hear any opposition to this?"

There was none and Frank walked up to the podium. Bill knew this was not usual protocol or procedure, but he also knew that churches do not follow proper procedures when there are two opposing sides with a lot of emotion. Besides, he trusted Frank completely.

The next motion from the floor came very abruptly, "I make a motion that we fire the preacher!"

From there things began getting out of control and very emotional. There were a few allegations that were minor at best.

They were small matters that were inflated to be as though they were major heresies, but certainly nothing substantial or incriminating. A few times people made personal statements against Bill and his family. When somebody in the audience made a rude comment about Bill's children, there were many loud objections.

Frank did a superb job at keeping things to a minimum, but Bill could see it was taking a toll on him.

Finally, the call came for a vote and a few men, whom Bill didn't recognize, stood and began handing out pencils and slips of paper. One member called for a point of order as to who would count the votes. Frank responded with a stern reply, "The Finance Committee will count the ballots."

It was wisdom from above. The entire finance committee had immaculate respect from just about everyone in the church and the community. This would be a fair count and everyone knew it. Bill couldn't help but notice that Sam sat in the back corner with a smug look on his face and never uttered a word. It's as though the others were doing all of his work for him.

For the first time, things began to quiet down as the ballots were passed down the end of each aisle. Ted, Henry and the others gathered them up and headed to the conference room.

Frank stood at the pulpit as they waited on the ushers to bring the results of the vote. As the noise of the crowd's whispering began to slowly rise with each passing moment, Frank saw a glimmer of a gash in the top of the pulpit where he realized the knife had been plunged. His heart began to hurt as he imagined the account of that night. He hurt for the church and for his pastor who had become like a son to him.

Frank reached into the front pocket of his overalls and discreetly pulled out his little bottle of Nitro Glycerin tablets. He slipped one under his tongue, seemingly without anyone noticing.

But someone did notice; his loving wife Marge.

She whispered a prayer for God to give him strength. Nobody knew how sick his heart really was and the last few weeks had taken a great toll on his overall health.

Finally, the committee came into the auditorium and the crowd became hushed. Ted walked up the steps to the podium and handed Frank the results. He whispered something to Frank before stepping back with his arms hanging down and hands clasped. As Ted informed him, Frank's head dropped down and he grabbed each side of the pulpit. The crowd began whispering to one another again.

"Ladies and gentleman, we are called back to order," Frank stated with his voice visibly shaking. You could hear his voice beginning to crack.

"The votes," Frank paused to gather himself, "are as follows..."

Good Things

During each of our pastorates, we enjoyed relationships with some wonderful and godly people. There were a lot of great times and we saw God move in miraculous ways. We saw many souls saved and several lives eternally changed. We have sustained friendships with many people whom we had met in the churches in which my husband and I ministered.

I am writing a second book and it will reveal wonderful things that God has done throughout the years. I will share more about a couple of awesome revivals and other stories from inside of the life of a pastor and his family. Some will be serious stories and some will be humorous. I truly desire to encourage pastors and their wives to keep on working for the Lord. You do make a difference!

Epilogue

Bill stood in the chilly breeze as the soft first snowflakes began to float and twirl to the ground. Looking down he began his farewell speech to his best friend.

"Well, Frank. I can't tell you enough how much you mean to me. I can never repay you for your friendship and everything you have taught me," Bill said.

"We've been down a long road together. After the overwhelming vote with more than two thirds desiring for me to remain as the pastor, I thought everything would just magically subside. But, it took a while and we lost quite a few members. I have certainly trusted God, but I must say there were some difficult times that made me wonder what God's plan was.

Now the church is twice the size it was before and we will have been here for nine years this October. The plan is to build a new worship center soon and a new children's department. God saw what we couldn't see and has blessed our labors and faith in Him.

I've got something to tell you though, Frank. God is calling us to a new work. With everything He has taught us here with your friendship and support, we hope to have an even greater journey in our new field. It's only a six hour drive so we can still come and visit occasionally. I will never forget you, dear friend. I believe the church is in good hands with some godly men and women now serving the church. I don't know if the church will ever know how much gratitude they owe you.

I love you, Frank. I hope you know that. I will never forget the way you stood up for the church and for me seven years ago. I am forever grateful to you."

Bill laid a single rose on Frank's headstone. He stood and stared down at the inscription, wiping the mist from his eyes. Bill pulled a handkerchief and dabbed his nose as he read the inscription aloud, "He gave the greater love."

As he turned to walk away he glanced over at the headstone next to Frank's and whispered, "I love you too Marge." Bill slowly walked out of the cemetery and to his car to start the next adventure in his life.

I can certainly say with confidence that I am grateful to God for the path we have traveled. As rocky and unstable as it has been at times, there is no greater joy in reflecting back to those dark moments and seeing the hand of God at work in every single circumstance. The wisdom we have gained has been invaluable not only to us, but to other ministers and their wives whom we have been blessed to encourage.

My hope is to encourage God's servants to stay faithful and focused on Jesus through all the strife and difficulties. Count it all joy as you experience the grace and power of God in your life. I am confident that you will also look back and see God's majestic hand at work through your difficult circumstances.

In the famous words of Winston Churchill, "Never, never, never, never, never, never give up!"

"²⁰Now the God of peace, that brought again from the dead our Lord Jesus, that great shepherd of the sheep, through the blood of the everlasting covenant, ²¹Make you perfect in every good work to do his will, working in you that which is wellpleasing in his sight, through Jesus Christ; to whom be glory for ever and ever. Amen."

~ Hebrews 13:20-21

Bibliography

[1]PEL Ministries, Rev. Lee Thomas, PO Box 1058, Westlake, LA 70669, 337-433-2663

[2]Zodhiates, Spiros; Baker, Warren: *The Complete Word Study Bible: King James Version*. Electronic Ed. Chattanooga: AMG Publishers, 2000, c1991, c1994

[3]Strong's Exhaustive Concordance is a concordance of the King James Bible (KJV) that was constructed under the direction of Dr. James Strong (1822–1894) and first published in 1890.

For more information about my ministry, please feel free to email me at: *encouragingpastorswives@gmail.com*. My desire is to encourage women, especially ministers' wives.

You can listen to my weekly radio segment "Encouraging Words For Ministers' Wives" online at *www.KELBradio.com*.

You are also welcome to email me to share stories or to make comments about this book.

Find me on Instagram@encouragingministerswives
You Tube: Danielle Richardson

DANIELLE RICHARDSON

www.ingramcontent.com/pod-product-compliance
Lightning Source LLC
Chambersburg PA
CBHW052139110526
44591CB00012B/1780